ARTSTRANDS
a program of individualized art instruction

Guy Hubbard   Enid Zimmerman
Indiana University

Waveland Press, Inc.
Prospect Heights, Illinois

For information about this book, write or call:

Waveland Press, Inc.
P.O. Box 400
Prospect Heights, Illinois 60070
(312) 634-0081

Cover photo courtesy of Leo Castelli Gallery, New York

Acknowledgements

This course began in 1971 as an instructional experiment designed to permit college students with little or no art background to enrich their education through art studies without having to concern themselves about competing with talented students planning to become professional artists. Support for this idea was given by faculty and administrators at Indiana University during the early years of the course until it became an established part of the undergraduate curriculum. Notable among these early supporters were Eugene Eoyang, Leo Solt, the late Robert C. Turner, K. Gene Faris, Thomas Schwen, and Thomas J. Hennessy.

At the daily operational level, the course succeeded because of contributions made by a dedicated group of supporters. Among the most notable of this group are Judy Kula, Sister Sarah Page, Trudy Shiel, Edith Curtice, Jeri Edwards, Carol Zelift, and William Broderick. Enid Zimmerman played an important part during the early development of the program and subsequently became the driving force behind all the later advances. I am indebted to her for her commitment and for the colleagueship we have shared while writing this book.

Guy Hubbard
Bloomington, Indiana
1982

Contents

Introduction

Textbooks help you learn something, and this one helps you learn the subject matter of art. A large part of this book involves making art, but it also includes learning information about art and forming your own opinions about works of art. Most art textbooks and most art courses are either about the history of art or they instruct people about one particular art form, such as painting or weaving. This book is different. It introduces you to numbers of different kinds of art and also to a wide range of ideas, information, and skills that are useful in several different areas of art.

This book is also different from other ones because you can use it to learn art in your own personal way. In most classes, everyone does more or less the same kind of thing. For example, when an instructor decides that a class of students should draw objects before they draw people, that is what happens. The authors decided to design art instruction where the students, rather than the teacher, would make most of the decisions about what to learn. This idea led to the development of a highly successful college course for which this book is the instructional manual.

Another important fact about this book and the course it serves is that the students are typical undergraduates. They enroll in the course because they want to advance their education by experiencing some of the various forms of art that exist. Few have had much art experience in school and many feel very self conscious about their lack of ability. The instruction that is included, therefore, is designed to enhance the education of interested college students whose art education up to this time has been neglected. In order to help students reach this goal, the lessons have been written in an effort to provide as many chances for success as possible. They have also been written so as to appeal to a wide range of student interests. Consequently, you should expect some lessons to appeal to you much more than others.

How To Use This Book

Because you make most of the choices about what you do in the course where this book is used, the instructor will usually serve more as a counselor than as a conventional teacher. And even though all final evaluations are made by the instructor, all decisions about evaluation will be based on "learning outcomes" that appear in each lesson — and only on those outcomes. Nothing is kept secret. As a result, your success is very much your own responsibility; and yet, because the lessons are reasonably simple, you have every opportunity to be successful.

You will face many questions when you open this book. Where shall I begin? How do I choose a lesson? Which of the hundred lessons should I choose? At first glance it seems that you have been given freedom of choice only for it to have been taken away because you do not know what to choose. But there are really several ways of getting started. The first and most common method is to look through the pages of the book. Some of the pictures will interest you more than others and cause you to pause for a moment. A catchy lesson title may then attract your attention and that, together with the pictures, may cause you to read the lesson introduction and perhaps the instructions about what to do. You may also find that the art materials list appeals to you; perhaps you would prefer to paint rather than to construct a piece of sculpture. However, the learning outcomes describe what really lies at the heart of each lesson. These outcomes are the reason why each of the lessons was written: they list art concepts and skills that you are to learn.

Each lesson includes all the parts that were just mentioned, and they appear in exactly the same locations in every lesson. As you look through the book, therefore, you can begin making some decisions about the art you would like to do. As you do this, you may also notice that

all one hundred lessons seem to be mixed together, randomly. Lesson One does not lead to Lesson Two, and Lesson 50 is not more difficult than Lesson 10. Moreover, lessons on drawing or sculpture are not grouped together. This random arrangement is deliberate and is intended to open up opportunities for making choices that are normally not available when instruction follows a prescribed path.

Another similar but less popular way of searching for what to do is to study the list of lesson titles at the beginning of the book. After each title is a brief description of the kind of art concepts and skills that are to be learned. When something interesting is discovered you can quickly turn to the lesson itself.

As you look through the book, you will soon discover that each lesson includes one or more diagrams, called "strands." Each strand is a group of related lessons selected from the one hundred in the book. Four lessons, chosen from the strand, are usually equal to one semester hour of credit in college courses. While every lesson is separate from all the others, every lesson is found in one or more strands. The strand is the instructional unit around which this book is organized. While you have considerable choice about the art you will do, you must follow the lessons in the order they appear in the strands. In this way, you avoid a completely free choice of lessons, that is no choice at all. Moreover, the lessons in the strands are related to each other in ways that may not be immediately apparent. In this way, you choose the direction of your art studies, and at the same time, receive direction for your art learning.

Four steps exist in each strand, as you can see from the diagram that appears at the end of this section. You always move from left to right, from the first step through the fourth one. Once again, however, you are given freedom of choice. At each step, you may choose from two or three lessons, with the result that many different alternative pathways are available in every strand. The number of choices becomes even greater when a particular lesson you want to do appears in more than one strand.

Just as the lessons are listed at the front of the book by title and brief description, so are the strands. Each strand has its own title followed by an abbreviated description of what kinds of instruction occur in it. However, as you look through the individual lessons you will also see the strand diagrams in which a particular lesson appears. In this way, you can find other ways to enter strands and to consider doing lessons that you had never thought you would enjoy.

To summarize, the individual lessons make up the smallest instructional units of the program. The learning outcomes present in each lesson establish the educational reasons for their existence. Related lessons and their outcomes are assembled into instructional sequences, called strands, that incorporate opportunities both for individual choice and instructional guidance.

The Strands

A strand consists of a group of related lessons where you are expected to begin with one of the choices available (arranged vertically) and then move to the second, third, and fourth sets of choices until a sequence of four lessons has been completed. The following step-by-step description, using an actual strand from the book, should make the procedure clear.

Strand 1. Title: *Visual Communication*

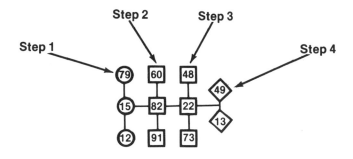

1. In this strand you must begin at Step 1 by executing Lesson 79, 15, or 12.

2. When you have completed all of the tasks listed in one of these lessons to the best of your ability, submit your work for evaluation.

3. When the work for the first lesson in Step 1 has been awarded a passing grade, select any one of the three lessons in Step 2 listed for the next stage in the strand, that is lesson 60, 82, or 91.

4. When the second lesson choice has been completed and has been awarded a passing grade, you will move to Step 3 and select Lesson 48, 22, or 73.

5. Finally, when the third lesson choice has received a satisfactory evaluation, you proceed to Step 4 and work on either Lesson 49 or 13 to complete the strand.

List of Lessons

Descriptions of Instruction for Each Strand

Strand   **Title**

1   *Visual Communication:* You are first introduced to lettering styles. In Step Two you are asked to think about the relationship between letters and other shapes. Step Three focuses on communicating meanings. The strand ends by bringing all of these components together in the creation of a poster or an illustration.

2   *Fantasy Messages:* The strand begins with experiments in the use of art materials and techniques to communicate feelings. Step Two directs you to the study of fantasy in art and elaborates on it in the following step in readiness for a final effort in the creation of fantastic art.

3   *Art Ideas from History:* The strand begins with studies of art from non-Western civilizations. Steps Two and Three include ancient art from the Western tradition followed by art from the Renaissance. Step Four requires that you use your history knowledge to create an art work of your own.

4   *The Power of Distortion:* Great master works, together with techniques such as simplification and exaggerated action poses are used as models for this strand. Steps Two and Three require you to concentrate on the artistic meanings to be communicated. The strand ends

7

with an assignment that calls for you to express emotional feelings.

5 *Fabric Art:* Each step in this strand focuses on a different form of textile design, beginning with stitchery and moving on to printing, collage, and appliqué. Step Three adds opportunities to learn about American fabric design, while Step Four introduces the idea of mixed media.

6 *Making Prints:* General design tasks lead to practice with simple printing techniques. Step Three requires you to think about ideas that might be used for creative printing; the strand ends with a design problem involving either block printing or stenciling.

7 *Drawing People:* The strand opens with lessons designed to give you practice in drawing rounded surfaces. This is followed first with drawing practice in the style of great artists and then drawing real people. The strand ends with a more expressive use of drawing.

8 *Art Ideas from Other Cultures:* Steps One and Two include basic drawing exercises. Step Three provides opportunities for studying Oriental, African, or North American Indian art. The strand ends with an emphasis on the use of symbols in art.

9 *Using Color to Show Distance:* This strand instructs you about how to show distance with color. You begin by working with subtle colors and blurred shapes and move from that to the use of brighter colors. Finally, you make use of colors that have special meaning for you.

10 *Deep Feelings:* Several methods of depicting specific moods can be chosen at Steps One and Two such as the use of grids and photographs. They are applied to solve problems in Steps Three and Four that call for the expression of deep feelings.

11 *Drawing Natural Objects:* First you draw objects and surfaces of objects, followed by experience in drawing art works from different periods in history. At Step Three you return again to making careful drawings of objects and to studying animal drawings. The concluding step uses the skills that have been developed earlier for drawing a plant or an animal.

12 *Techniques of Using Paint:* Step One opens with lessons designed to develop your skill in using paint. Steps Two and Three give practice in using paint and an opportunity to think about how to use various painting techniques. The strand ends with lessons where you use these techniques to communicate different artistic messages.

13 *Adding and Subtracting in Art:* The strand begins with simple modelling and carving techniques. Steps Three and Four introduce more complicated techniques and also include sculptural problems from history and architecture.

14 *Dominance in Art:* A fundamental art principal is that one part of a work should stand out clearly. This strand includes the principle of dominance in each of the lessons. At each step, the assignments become more complex and more abstract.

15 *Art and Geometry:* Lettering, stitchery, and some kinds of Indian art often use geometric shapes. After working on lessons where you study geometrical designs, you move on to more contemporary art in which the main emphasis is on designing with geometric shapes.

16 *Appreciating Sculpture:* Step One includes simple casting and carving exercises. The Step Two drawing assignments and the Step Three historical studies prepare you for more advanced sculptural lessons in Step Four.

17 *Recent Art History:* This strand includes a mixture of lessons, some of which require you to write essays and others require you to produce art. All of the lessons ask you to study art works by distinguished artists.

18 *Decorating Flat Surfaces:* The strand begins with some exercises where you study flat shapes and patterns. The lessons in Steps Two and Three include instructions on different art forms that concentrate on designing flat shapes. The strand ends with opportunities for creative expression using flat shapes exclusively.

19 *Rhythmic Movement:* You are introduced to the fundamental principal of rhythm in Step One. It is extended at Step Two to include rhythmic artistic styles and is further elaborated at Step Three. You end the strand by creating a highly personal picture where you develop a rhythmic theme.

20 *Portraits that Show Personality:* The strand begins with studies of faces followed by exercises on drawing faces. In Step Three you work at including facial expressions and end the strand with personal creations that capture people's personalities.

21   *Perspective Drawing:* Step One includes a general introduction to drawing. Steps Two and Three introduce you to one and two point perspective. The strand concludes with advanced applications of perspective drawing.

22   *Expressing Great Ideas:* This strand offers opportunities for you to explore a variety of topics that have inspired artists. The strand starts with more obvious topics and moves at each step toward more poetic and emotional themes.

23   *Searching for Artistic Ideas:* Steps One and Two provide visual ideas. Steps Three and Four enrich the previous lessons by including sculpture, the history of art, and the theme of human weakness.

24   *The Middle Ages and the Renaissance:* After completing introductory lessons about studying historical art works, you make drawings of masterpieces from the Middle Ages or the Renaissance. In the last two steps of the strand, you have opportunities either to continue the historical studies or to apply ideas from history to create your own art.

25   *Simplification:* Steps One and Two move from careful drawings of historical art to more recent art where simplification is stressed. Step Three provides opportunities for you to explore simplification in designs while Step Four asks you to explore more abstract ideas.

26   *The Art of Architecture:* Steps One and Two include basic drawing exercises that emphasize perspective. Step Three asks you to study the appearance and the construction of buildings. The strand ends with a choice of architectural design problems.

27   *The Vitality of Lines:* You are introduced to the basic element of line in this strand through drawing exercises and design assignments. After studying drawings made by great artists, and also learning that lines can be used in sculpture, you create an art work of your own that reveals your powers of observation.

28   *Symbolism in Art:* Exercises in Step One using words and patterns lead to studies of historic artistic symbols and fantasy. In Step Four, you apply your knowledge of symbolism in your own artistic creation.

1 colors can express moods

Color is one of the most effective ways of expressing a mood. The lyric of one song, "Blue, blue, my love is blue," is in direct contrast to another, "A rainbow shines in my window, my love loves me." A gray day rolls over us like a fog in San Francisco, silent and eerie, as opposed to the white heat of the sand of a Jamaican beach. In this lesson you will express a mood using the art medium of paper collage.* Artists use shapes, colors, and textures of paper to create collages that express moods and feelings.

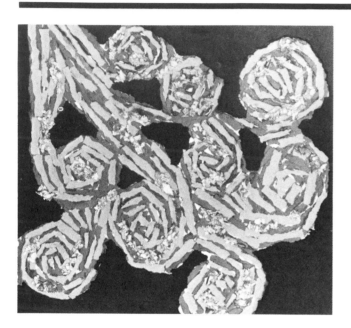

Student paper collages.

Instructions:

1. Make a collection of many varieties of papers. Include shades of colored construction paper, newspaper, plain and patterned wrapping paper, slick surfaced pages from magazines, spongy paper towels, as well as your choice of other interesting kinds of paper.

2. Choose a particular piece of music that appeals to you such as a folksong, Beethoven's "Pastorale" symphony, "Switched on Bach," or a rock piece. Communicate the mood you have chosen through the choice of colors, textures, and patterns from your collection of papers.

3. Different kinds of music have rhythms that vary throughout a particular piece. Some of these rhythms are stronger than others. The main part of your design should focus on one strong rhythm from your chosen piece of music. For example, you might use sweeping rounded shapes, small geometric shapes, or combinations of large and small shapes to depict a strong rhythm. This dominant rhythm should be the focus of attention in your collage. The design for the collage should be non-objective, that is it should not contain real-life objects.

4. Once your design is complete, use rubber cement to attach the cut and torn papers to a 12" × 18" base of stiff paper or cardboard. The entire surface of the base of the collage should be covered with pieces of paper.

    Attach a label to the back, naming the piece of music you have chosen.

5. Submit for evaluation the finished paper collage based on a mood expressed in a piece of music.

Learning Outcomes:

1. List various types of paper materials that can be glued to a surface to produce a collage.
2. Explain how different rhythms can be expressed through the collage medium.*
3. Make a 12" x 18" collage expressing the mood of one strong movement of a piece of music.

Suggested Materials:

Stiff paper or cardboard, 12" × 18"; various colors and types of paper; scissors; rubber cement

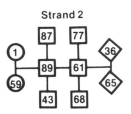

Strand 2

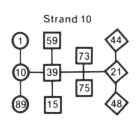

Strand 10

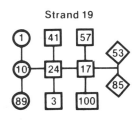

Strand 19

Student paper collage.

2

extending a photograph

In many drawings, paintings, advertisements, and photographs, people are depicted in specific settings such as gardens, museums, and living rooms. The people together with the setting tell a story. Without the background setting, it might be difficult to understand the people's actions.

Sometimes you may look at a photograph and imagine what it would look like if the setting were extended to include more details, objects, and other persons. In this lesson, you will use your imagination and draw additions around a photograph so that a whole story is told.

Instructions:

1. Find a black and white photograph in a magazine or newspaper that contains people in action with buildings around them.

2. Use rubber cement to adhere the photograph to a larger piece of white drawing paper. Extend the photograph in at least two directions by drawing additions to the photograph. Your additions should tell a larger story than the one that was shown in the original photograph. For example, a robber can be added to a peaceful scene outside a bank. Match style, shading, darks, lights, textures, etc. with the original photograph. Check to make sure that the perspective* of the buildings in the extended parts is accurate.

3. Submit for evaluation your drawing of a photograph extended in at least two directions.

Christie Park: Courtesy of the artist.   Three-part photo collage.

12

Learning Outcomes:

1. List characteristics of your extensions that match the original photograph.
2. Explain how your extensions tell a more complete story than the original photograph.
3. Draw extensions in at least two directions to a photograph of people in action and buildings which add content and meaning to the original.

2

Suggested Materials:

White drawing paper; pencils and eraser; scissors; rubber cement; black and white photograph

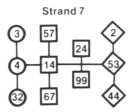

Strand 7

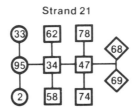

Strand 21

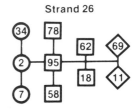

Strand 26

Finished student extension of a photograph.

Original photograph.

Student drawing with the photograph removed.

13

3

figures in action

The tilt of the torso, the angle of the hip, or the bend of an arm or leg can all convey some sort of action or tension. Very seldom do we see human figures that are stiff or still. These suggestions of movement convey the variety of actions that the human body can perform.

In this lesson, you will have the opportunity to use a photograph to help you draw an accurately proportioned figure in an action pose.

Instructions:

1. Find a photograph of a person engaged in strenuous action. It could be a sprinter, a dancer, a basketball player, or a gymnast. The view you choose should show the entire body.

2. Make two quick outline sketches* on a piece of paper to show the main angles taken by the body parts. Do not copy the photograph in detail. Try to capture the vigorous movement of the person.

3. Choose the sketch you think best captures the action of the pose. Draw the pose again and this time make it larger than the photograph. Include correct angles of body parts and shading in this final drawing. See page 223 for a checklist of body proportions to help you draw your figure accurately.

4. Submit for evaluation all preliminary sketches, your final drawing of a figure in action, and the photograph you used.

Finished student action drawing.

Learning Outcomes:

1. List the typical proportions of the human body.
2. Explain how the human body can be drawn to depict its movement in space.
3. From a photograph, draw a full length figure of a vigorously active person with accurate proportional relations and shading.

Suggested Materials:

Drawing paper; pencil; photograph of a figure in an action pose

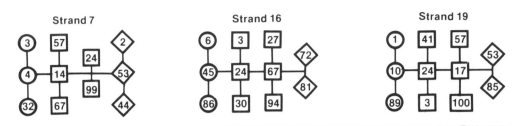

Strand 7   Strand 16   Strand 19

Francisco de Goya (1746-1828). *Three Men Digging.* Brush & wash. The Metropolitan Museum of Art, Harris Brisbane Dick Fund.

4

half faces

Many times artists use photographs, or parts of photographs, to help them complete their drawings. If someone helps you do a difficult task by doing half of it, the other half often seems a lot easier. In this lesson, half the work will be done for you, leaving only half for you to do.

Student work: half photograph and half drawing.

Student full face drawing.

Instructions:

1. Select a large black and white magazine photograph of the full front view of a person's head. Be sure to select a photograph that is a full front view. Cut the photograph exactly in half vertically (i.e. down an imaginary center line through the nose and between the eyes). Each half will be approximately the same because faces are almost symmetrical, that is, exactly the same on both sides of the center line. Use rubber cement to attach one half of the photograph in the center of a sheet of white drawing paper.

2. Use the cemented half picture as a guide to help you draw the missing half accurately. The unused half of the photograph can be studied to see how the features, hairstyle, shape of the head, etc. are formed. Draw the missing half of the head with a fairly soft pencil, making it look as much like the other half as possible. Pay attention to dark and light areas of the face. Observe the contour (i.e. outline) of the shape of the face. Use shading* to make the face look solid. See page 223 for a checklist of facial proportions.

4. After the drawing of the face is complete, take another sheet of paper and draw the entire front view of the face yourself. The experience of drawing the half face should help you draw the whole face. Check to make sure your symmetry is accurate.

5. Submit the unused half of the original black and white photograph, the cemented half photograph and a half drawing, and the full face drawing.

Learning Outcomes:

1. Define symmetry in reference to balance.
2. Explain why it is easier to draw a face if half a face is provided as a guide than if no guide is provided.
3. Draw both half a face to match a photograph of the other half and the whole of a full front portrait showing accurate proportion, contour, and shading.

4

Suggested Materials:

White drawing paper; soft pencil; scissors; rubber cement; magazine photographs of a full front view of a person's head

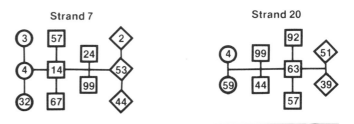

Student work: half photograph and half drawing.

Student full face drawing.

17

5 the seven deadly sins

The seven deadly sins are themes well suited for pictorial expression. They have been depicted in many different ways by artists throughout history. These sins are pride, covetousness (greed), lust (usually sexual), envy, gluttony (usually including drunkenness), anger, and sloth (laziness).

In this lesson, you are to depict one of the seven deadly sins in a way that best expresses your interpretation of that sin. The choice of shapes, lines, textures, etc. will be your own. However, you are to use watercolor or tempera paints and to follow special instructions about the use of color.

Instructions:

1. Plan a picture, on a 12" × 18" sheet of paper, for a painting of your interpretation of one of the seven deadly sins. Draw a large, dominant image to emphasize the theme of the sin such as burning flames for the sin of anger. Use several other images that relate to, but are less important than the dominant theme. Such images are described in art as subordinate. For example, you might use shooting rockets in the background of a picture about anger.

2. Paint the picture you have planned by using a restricted range of colors, that is, by using a limited color palette. Think of one color that best expresses your interpretation of the sin you have chosen. Use this color and variations of it to paint the dominant* parts of the picture.

To draw attention to certain parts of the picture, use the complementary color to the color you have just chosen. The complementary will be opposite the first color on the color wheel. Thus, if the main color is red, the complement will be green, if the main color is blue, the complement will be orange, and if the main color is yellow, the complement will be purple. If you use tempera paint you may wish to add black and white to make colors lighter and darker. For transparent water colors, use black to make colors darker and water to make colors lighter.

3. Submit for evaluation a 12" × 18" tempera or watercolor painting of one of the deadly sins.

Peter Brueghel [the Elder] (1525/30 - 1569). *Envy — One of the Seven Vices.* Engraving. The Metropolitan Museum of Art, Harris Brisbane Dick Fund.

Learning Outcomes:

1. Explain why artists use a limited palette as a restriction on colors.
2. List the color and its complement you chose.
3. Paint a 12" x 18" tempera or watercolor picture that represents your idea of one of the seven deadly sins using dominant and subordinate* images.

5

Suggested Materials:

Paper (approximately 12" × 18"); pencil; eraser; paints; brushes; mixing tray; paper towels; water

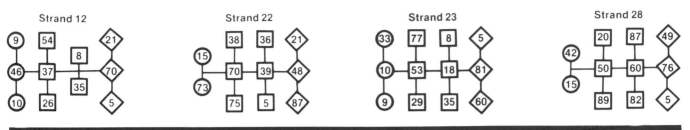

Strand 12 · Strand 22 · Strand 23 · Strand 28

Henry Koerner (1915 -) *Vanity Fair.* Oil on board. Collection of Whitney Museum of American Art, New York.

6   hand sculpture

Artists use two main ways of making sculpture. One way requires adding pieces together in the additive* method. The other requires cutting pieces away in the subtractive* method. The process of cutting away is called carving. This lesson asks that you carve a piece of sculpture where your sense of touch will tell you when it is successful.

Instructions:

1. Cut into a fairly large block of wax, soft wood, or plaster — or anything else that can be carved easily. Carve the block so that your hands fit around the solid form in a pleasing way. Be careful about cutting too much away. You can rarely glue pieces back on that have been removed by accident.

2. While carving the piece, give thought to ways in which the surface can be made pleasing to touch. Some parts may be rough while others may be smooth. Alternatively, special patterns* may be applied. Finish the surface* so that the entire object feels good and looks good. The object should not represent anything in real life.

3. Submit for evaluation a carved block with pleasing surfaces.

Barbara Hepworth (1903 - 1975). *Oval Sculpture.* Polished bronze, cast from a plaster original. Barbara Hepworth Museum, St. Ives, England.

Learning Outcomes:

1. Describe two basic ways that sculpture is made.
2. Explain why the sense of touch is as important for evaluating sculpture as the sense of sight.
3. Carve a solid block that feels pleasing and shows varied surface treatments and does not resemble anything in real life.

6

Suggested Materials:

Surface treatments: polish, sandpaper, paint, felt markers, etc.; carving instrument: knife, rasp, etc.; a fairly large block of wax, wood, plaster, styrofoam, etc.

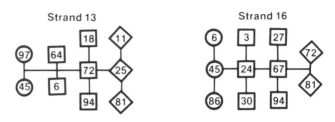

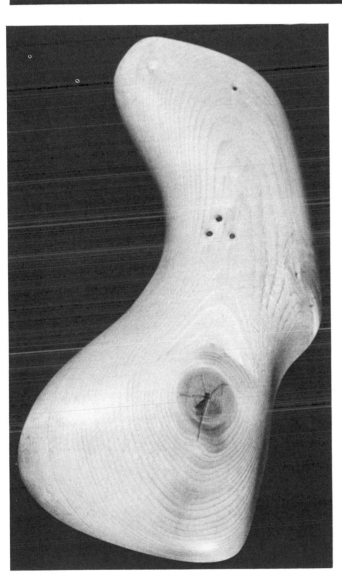

Student carved wood hand sculpture.

Student carved plaster hand sculpture.

21

7

flat sided objects

Light rays travel in straight lines. These rays bounce off flat surfaces*, called planes, at the same angle they hit. Flat sided objects, such as furniture, buildings, and boxes have edges or corners where flat sides meet. Sides of flat sided objects that face the light directly reflect whatever light is available to a maximum. They are brighter than surfaces that do not face the light directly and consequently reflect less light.

The corners and edges, where planes meet, are easy to see because changes in reflected light are very evident. Each plane is darker or lighter than the one next to it. Artists are sensitive to these differences in lightness and darkness and show them in their work. This lesson offers the opportunity to study and to draw the effects created by light as it strikes flat sided objects.

Instructions:

1. Arrange a group of solid, flat-sided objects in a pleasing way. Alternatively, find a view of some buildings that appeals to you. Make sure the objects in the group are lit from a single direct light source such as a lamp, window, or strong sunlight.

2. Draw the shapes of the flat sided objects in the group you have chosen. Check your drawing for correct perspective, accurate details, and proportion* of objects to each other.

3. Shade all planes to show correct amounts of lightness and darkness. Surfaces facing the light source will be lighter than those facing away. Very few parts will be completely black or white. Most planes will be some shade of gray. Pay attention to shadows under objects and to places where objects overlap each other. Draw objects that are close to you in greater detail than those that are farther away.

4. Submit for evaluation a shaded* drawing of flat sided objects lit from a single light source.

Student drawing of a group of flat sided objects.

Charles Sheeler (1883-1965). *Bucks County Barn.* Crayon on paper. Collection of the Whitney Museum of American Art, New York.

Learning Outcomes:

1. Define plane in référence to a flat surface.
2. Explain how surfaces facing a light source are different from those turned away.
3. Make a drawing of a group of flat sided objects in correct perspective, with accurate detail, proportion, and shading.

7

Suggested Materials:

Drawing paper, at least 9'' × 12''; fairly soft leaded pencils; eraser; flat sided objects

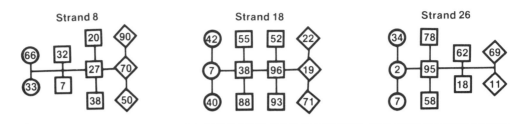

Strand 8

Strand 18

Strand 26

Moshe Safdie. *Habitat 67* (1967). Department of public relations, City of Montreal, Canada.

Light and shadow on the flat surfaces of modern apartments.

23

8

looking at paintings

You may have wanted to visit art museums in your community or nearby, but other things happen and you never seem to get a chance to go. This lesson offers you the opportunity to go to an art museum with a specific purpose in mind. You are asked to visit the museum and to look carefully at the paintings in the collection. You are then to answer questions about the paintings you saw from a prepared set of directions. This lesson will help you to learn to look at paintings by focusing upon specific features and art elements.

Instructions:

1. Visit a museum in your community that contains a collection of paintings. Read the following directions and try to find paintings that match the criteria in the directions. For each painting you discuss give the title, artist's name, and the date the painting was created. Keep your statements fairly brief.

a) A painter can apply pigment (paint) in different ways. Paint that is very thin and looks watery creates a wash. Paint that is applied to create a thick textured surface is called impasto. Describe how pigment is applied in a painting that uses the wash method. Describe the painted surface* in a painting that uses the impasto method.

b) A medium is any material used for expression in art. Describe the materials in a painting that use one medium, or several media, in addition to paint.

c) Sometimes you can tell from the way a painting appears what tools or materials the artist used to apply paint to a canvas surface. Describe application of paint in a painting or paintings that looks as if it was created with a small brush, with a large brush, or by some other method.

d) You will notice that colors in some paintings are so bright they almost hurt your eyes. We call these colors intense. Colors in other paintings appear less intense and may even be quiet or dull. Describe a painting with dull colors. Describe one with intense colors. Describe one in which dull and intense colors contrast.

e) Some painters use colors realistically while others do not concern themselves with depicting color this way. Describe how color is used realistically in a painting. Describe how colors that do not appear true to life are used in another painting.

f) Some artists use recognizable people, objects, and scenes in their paintings. Some of these paintings tell a story. Describe a painting in detail that has subject matter* that depicts an event or displays a particular mood.

g) Non-objective paintings are composed of art elements such as color, line, shape, and texture but do not portray recognizable objects. Describe a painting that has art elements but does not contain any recognizable content.

2. Submit for evaluation answers to seven sets of directions about paintings in a museum.

Charles Demuth (1883-1935). *I Saw the Figure Five in Gold.* Oil on board. The Metropolitan Museum of Art, The Alfred Stieglitz Collection.

Learning Outcomes:

1. List seven classifications used to describe paintings, i.e., paint application and subject matter.
2. Describe paintings in a museum collection by writing answers to seven sets of directions.

Suggested Materials:

Writing paper; typing paper; paper and pen; typewriter

8

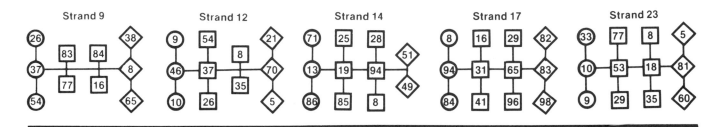

Graham Sutherland (1903 -). *Thorn Trees.* Oil on board. Albright-Knox Art Gallery, Buffalo, New York.

9

rainy landscapes

Poetry and prose can communicate a rainy feeling. "Here Comes that Rainy Day Feeling Again" is the name of a popular song. Pictures can also communicate feelings that are rainy, blurry, and misty. One art medium that is particularly suitable for creating a feeling of saturation is transpaprent watercolor because it can be applied in a wet manner. Watercolor is sold in tubes or small cakes of solid or nearly solid color. In this lesson, you will keep a watery, rainy feeling in mind as you experiment with watercolors and create a landscape* painting.

Student watercolor landscape.

Instructions:

1. Fill at least four 9" × 12" sheets of white paper with watercolor experiments. To create large areas of color use the side of the brush; use the point of the brush to create lines. Experiment on paper that is wet and on paper that is dry to create different watercolor effects. Explore the effects created by the use of various quantities of water from the driest possible to very watery. Mix a variety of different colors together. Instead of using white paint to lighten colors, add more water.

2. When you have developed an understanding of watercolor techniques, draw lightly with pencil to plan a real or imaginary landscape. Use a 12" × 18" sheet of paper. Include a foreground*, middleground*, and background* in your drawing (see diagram on page 223) as well as some objects of special interest.

3. Think about color and color application that express a watery, rainy feeling. Paint a watercolor of a landscape with a rainy day mood.

4. Submit for evaluation the four 9" × 12" experimental sheets and your finished 12" × 18" watercolor landscape painting.

Charles Burchfield (1893-1967). *An April Mood*. Watercolor. Collection of Whitney Museum of American Art, New York. Gift of Mr. and Mrs. Lawrence A. Fleischman.

Learning Outcomes:

1. List several watercolor techniques that can be used to create a rainy mood in a landscape painting.

2. Explain your choice of watercolor techniques that are most applicable for creating a rainy day mood in a landscape painting.

3. Make four 9" × 12" watercolor experiments and create a 12" × 18" watercolor painting of a landscape that communicates a rainy day mood.

Suggested Materials:

Watercolor paper, 9" × 12", 12" × 18"; watercolor paint; brushes—large soft brush and a small soft brush; mixing tray; paper towels; water

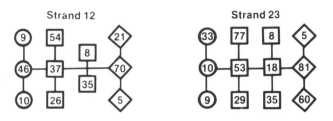

Norman Daly (1911 -). *Mountain Storm*. Watercolor. Allen Memorial Art Museum, Oberlin College. Gift of Donald Love.

10 the power of emotional feeling

Love, hate, anger, jealousy, and fear are a few of the powerful emotions that artists portray through their art. Each of us is susceptible to emotional feelings and each feeling brings different images to mind. In this lesson, you will paint your interpretation of the moment when a specific emotion is at its highest.

Instructions:

1. Focus your attention on a specific powerful emotion that you have experienced in the past. On four 8" x 10" sheets of white drawing paper rapidly paint, with tempera, as many different interpretations as you can of this powerful emotion. Use color, line, shape, and subject matter to communicate the emotion you have chosen.

2. Select the painting sketch* you think is best and develop it into a 12" x 18" tempera paint-

ing that expresses the heightened emotion you focused upon. Think carefully, as you paint, so as to make the most effective use of feeling, subject matter*, shape, line, and color.

3. Submit for evaluation four 8" x 10" painted sketches and the finished 12" x 18" tempera painting that express the power of an emotional feeling.

George Tooker (1920 -). *Government Bureau.* Tempera on board. The Metropolitan Museum of Art. George A. Hearn Fund.

Learning Outcomes:

1. Explain why heightened emotions are often depicted in art works.
2. Explain why the sketch you chose better represents a particular emotion than the others.
3. Make a 12'' x 18'' tempera painting based upon the best of four 8'' x 10'' sketches.

10

Suggested Materials:

Paper, 8'' x 10'' and 12'' x 18''; tempera paints; brushes; mixing tray; paper towels; water

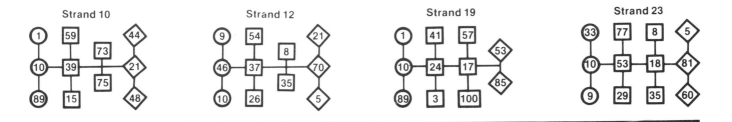

Strand 10   Strand 12   Strand 19   Strand 23

Oskar Kokoschka. *The Wind's Bride* (1914), Kunstmuseum, Basel, Switzerland.

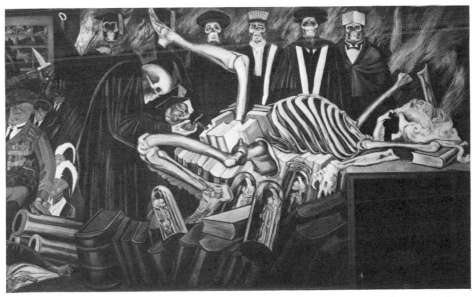

Jose Clemente Orozco (1883-1949). *Gods of the Modern World.* Fresco. Panel 12 of the murals in the Baker Library, Dartmouth College.

11 architectural design

Architecture is like sculpture in that it should be good to look at when viewed from different positions. But buildings are extremely expensive to erect. To help a prospective owner understand how a completed building will look, an architect will often make a model before the actual construction begins. Then, everyone involved can be sure that the building will look the way that is desired.

In this lesson you have the opportunity to design a building and to make a model of it.

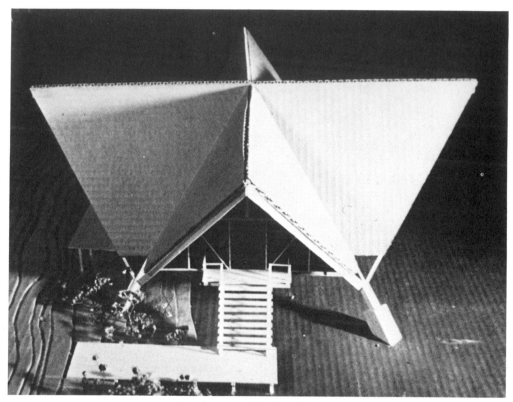

Student model of a building.

Instructions:

1. Visit your local library and search through architectural books and magazines for examples of building designs you think are very creative. Make drawings or xerox copies of the examples that appeal to you most. Some ideas may be very modern and others may be based on older styles.

2. Draw a design for a building. It should have a specific function, such as an airport terminal, a vacation home, a sports arena, a church, or a clubhouse. The ideas collected from books and magazines should provide useful ideas, but your design should be very much your own.

3. Make a model of your design. Suitable materials include foamcore, cardboard, balsa wood, and blocks of wood. Finish the model as perfectly as possible with all the details you would actually see. You may want to include such things as balconies, swimming pools, windows, steps, and doors.

4. Submit for evaluation the model and all the sketches*, xerox copies of buildings selected from library books and magazines as well as the preliminary drawings made for the design.

Learning Outcomes:

1. Explain why architects frequently make models of proposed buildings In addition to drawings.
2. Describe the purpose of the building you designed.
3. Make a detailed model of a building, based upon a drawing, using materials of your choice.

Suggested Materials:

Cardboard; pen and ink; scissors; glue; cutting knife; pins; clay and associated supplies; balsa wood; newspaper (to protect table top).

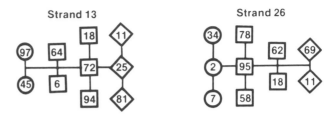

Student models of buildings.

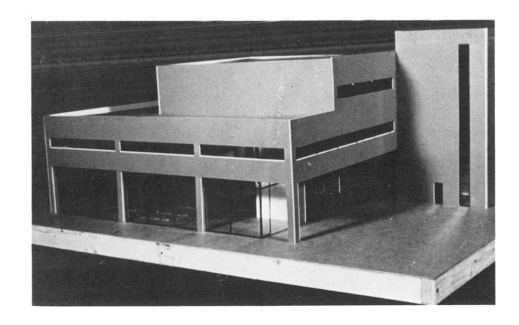

12

practicing lettering

Scribes handlettered all the words found in manuscripts written in the Middle Ages. It was not until the 15th century that printing was done where each letter was a separate piece. Before that, the whole page of a book was printed from a single piece of carved wood. Movable type made printing much quicker and cheaper than before, and it soon replaced handlettering. Today, over 10,000 different designs of movable type exist. Letters can have a personality of their own and their shapes alone can convey a variety of messages. Words formed from differently shaped letters are used by designers as important elements in their graphic work. In this lesson, you will choose a lettering design that appeals to you and letter a complete alphabet with that design.

Instructions:

1. Find a book that contains examples of different designs of lettering. Choose an alphabet with capital letters, in a style* that appeals to you. Study the letters. The letters may be simple and uniform in width, thick and thin with horizontal strokes, slanted and made to simulate handwriting, or to resemble handlettering of scribes. Notice if the letters are plain or decorated, large or small, thick or thin, straight edged or narrow, vertical or slanted, outlined or solid. Also, notice whether the letters are close together or far apart.

2. Before you begin handlettering the alphabet, remember the width of the letters should all be the same except for M and W. These are 1½ times the width of the other letters. The letter T should be ½ the width of the other letters. Use the same mid-line height for the center of all letters.

3. In a size larger than the original, accurately copy your chosen alphabet. Be sure to rule all guide lines lightly in pencil before forming the letters. You may use pen and black ink or a felt tipped pen to letter. Try to make the letters uniform in style so they all appear to go together.

4. Submit for evaluation a photocopy of the original capital letter alphabet and your copy of this alphabet.

Student copies of capital letter alphabets.

ABCDEFGHI
JKLMNOPQ
RSTUVWXYZ

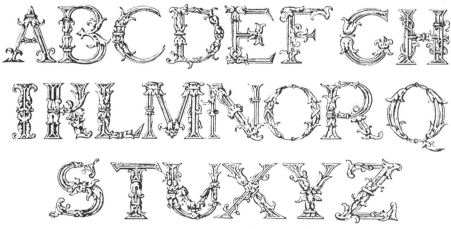

Ornamental alphabet, England, 1490.

32

Learning Outcomes:

1. List and describe some differences between lettering styles.
2. List characteristics, such as size and shape, of your chosen lettering style.
3. Hand-letter, with accuracy, an alphabet in capital letters, in ink, that is larger in size than the original alphabet from which it was copied.

Suggested Materials:

White drawing paper; pencil and eraser; pen and black ink or black felt tipped pen; ruler

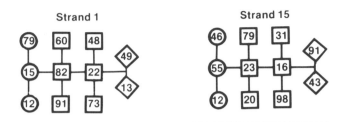

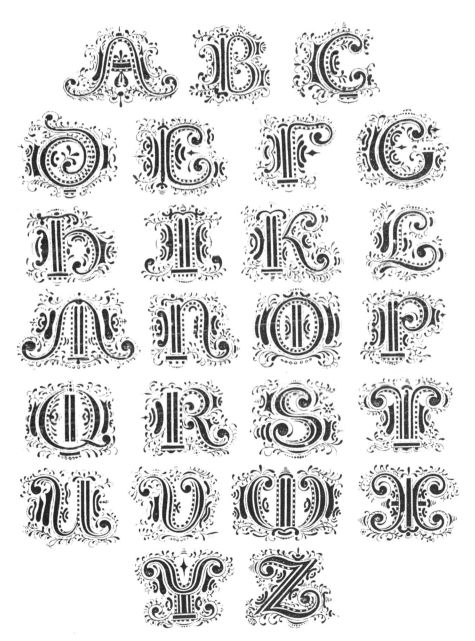

Ornamental alphabet, Austria, 18th century.

13

art in illustration

For centuries, books have contained pictures or designs, in addition to the written text. These pictures or designs either decorated the book or illustrated some part of a story. The size of a book's pages limits what artists can do; yet, some artists prefer to create book illustrations rather than to create other kinds of art work.

Here is an opportunity to illustrate a favorite poem or story. To create your combination of words and pictures, you can choose from a variety of art media.*

Student illustrations of poems.

Instructions:

1. Think of yourself as an illustrator who has been given the responsibility of illustrating a poetry or story book. Select a poem or part of a story you like. Ask yourself about the feelings and images it evokes.

2. In pencil, plan a composition*, for a single or double page, to illustrate the poem or part of the story you have selected. You may use places and events in the story as inspiration. In your plan, the illustration and the text should fit together to form a unified composition. Remember, one single image can sometimes evoke the feeling of a poem rather than many detailed small images.

3. Design a finished single or double page illustration for your chosen poem or story book. Use your pencil plan as a basis for your design. You may use either drawings or paintings to illustrate the text. You need not print the poem or part of the story. You may photocopy or type the written text and incorporate it into your design.

4. Submit for evaluation your plan and a finished single or double page drawing or painting, including written text, that illustrates a poem or part of a story.

Learning Outcomes:

1. Explain how illustrators design illustrations that go with written words.
2. Explain how an illustration of a poem or story can be made to fit together with the written text to form a unified composition.
3. Draw or paint an illustration for a poem or part of a story in which the words and pictures fit together to form a unified design.

13

Suggested Materials:

Paper; pencils; tempera or watercolor; brushes; mixing tray; scissors; rubber cement; water, paper towels

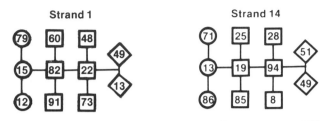

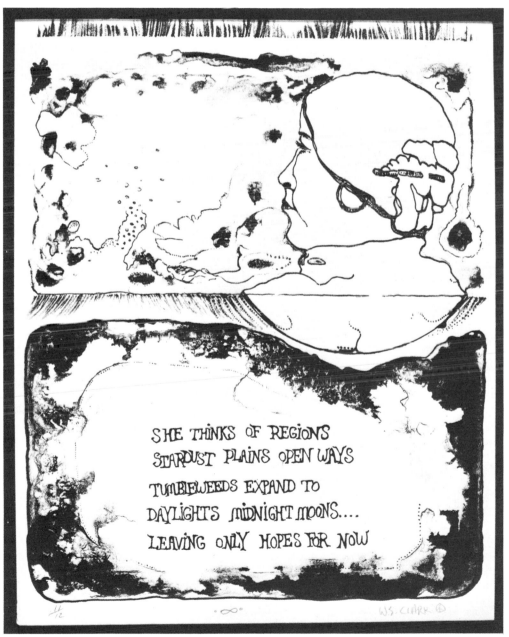

W. Stephen Clark: Courtesy of the artist.

Illustration with text.

35

14

leonardo da vinci

Leonardo Da Vinci (1452-1519) lived during a period marked by a revival of interest in the arts and classical learning that had largely been ignored or forgotten since the days of ancient Greece and Rome. He personified the spirit of insatiable curiosity that characterized great thinkers and artists of the Renaissance. As a painter, sculptor, inventor, biologist, astronomer, engineer, architect, and mathematician, Da Vinci made unique contributions to the culture of his time. His drawings of portraits and figures are outstanding and have as much appeal for people today as they did when he was alive.

Instructions:

1. Da Vinci did many realistic and caricature drawings of people. One way to learn about drawing and how it is created is to go through the same process that artists do when they draw. Choose two reproductions of drawings by Da Vinci, either portraits or full length figures, that appeal to you. His work is represented in art books in most libraries, so you should have no difficulty finding his drawings. Try to find excellent reproductions of Da Vinci's drawings.

2. Carefully study the contours*, proportions*, shading*, line quality, and details in Da Vinci's drawings. Make two drawings of the Da Vinci drawings you have chosen to study. Render all proportions, shading, lines, and details as accurately as possible so they closely resemble Da Vinci's. When drawing, constantly refer to the Da Vinci originals. Use good quality drawing paper and soft lead pencils for this assignment. Do not trace the Da Vinci's. See page 223 for checklists of body and facial proportions.

3. Submit for evaluation photocopies of the two Da Vinci drawings of portraits or full length figures and your two drawings based on them.

Student drawing based on a drawing by Leonardo da Vinci.

Learning Outcomes:

1. Describe how Da Vinci personified the spirit of the Renaissance in Italy.
2. Explain why Da Vinci's drawings are excellent examples for the study of portraits and full length figures.
3. Make accurate drawings of two Da Vinci portraits or figures.

14

Suggested Materials:
Drawing paper; soft lead pencil

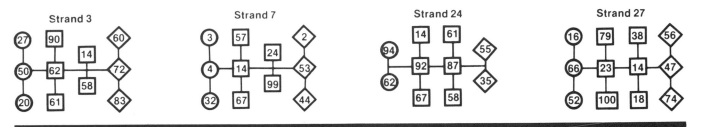

Strand 3

27 · 90 · · 60
50 · 62 — 14 — 72
· · 58
20 · 61 · · 83

Strand 7

3 · 57 · · 2
4 · 14 — 24 — 53
· · 99
32 · 67 · · 44

Strand 24

· 14 · 61 ·
94 · 92 — 87 — 55
62 · · · 35
· 67 · 58 ·

Strand 27

16 · 79 · 38 · 56
66 · 23 — 14 — 47
52 · 100 · 18 · 74

Student drawing based on a drawing by Leonardo da Vinci.

Have you ever noticed the different kinds of lettering that appear on posters, billboards, record albums, and movie advertisements? Many times, the style of letters conveys the feeling the advertiser wants you to associate with the product. If an advertisement contains the word *weak* the letters look limp and pathetic. Can you imagine how words such as *brutal, hysterical,* or *delicate* might look?

Detail of student words that convey different meanings.

Instructions:

1. Select at least 20 words, each of which conveys a very different meaning to you.

2. For each word, design a style* of lettering that illustrates your interpretation of that word. The colors, lines, and shapes of the letters should correspond with the meanings of the words. Do not depend on props for meanings such as a heart shape for the letter *O* in the word *love* or a smiling face for the letter *A* in the word *happy.*

3. Make sure all words are carefully lettered and easy to read. Arrange the words attractively on the sheet of paper so that all the colors, lines, and shapes go together to give unity to the composition*. Use any appropriate drawing or painting medium for the words in your composition.

4. Submit for evaluation, on a 9" x 12" sheet of paper, 20 words, created in your choice of medium, that convey different word meanings.

Learning Outcomes:

1. Explain why designers often invent lettering styles to convey particular feelings expressed by words they illustrate.
2. Design, on a 9" x 12" sheet of paper, 20 words that convey different meanings through the choice of letter shapes, colors, and lines.

Suggested Materials:

Paper, 9" x 12"; pencils; pen and ink; felt pens; crayons; paints, brushes, etc.

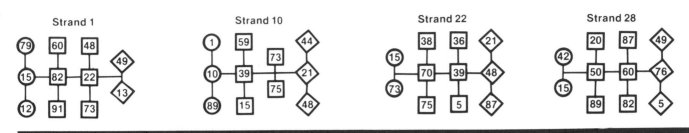

Strand 1 · Strand 10 · Strand 22 · Strand 28

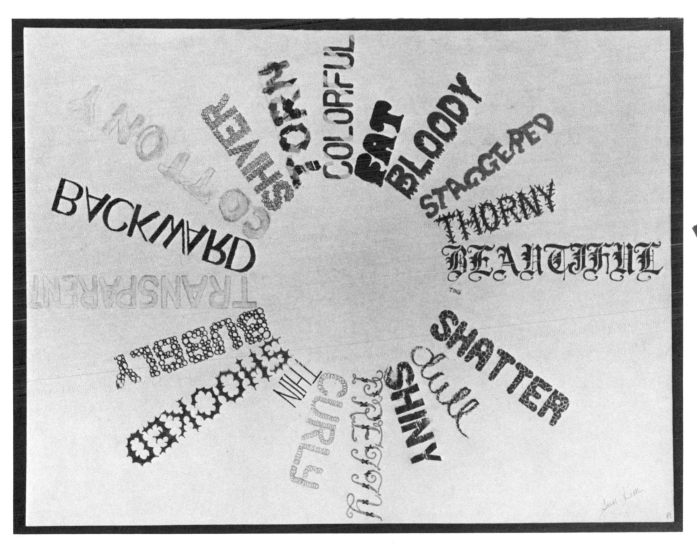

Twenty words that convey different meanings.

16

cézanne

For many people, all painting and sculpture that does not look realistic is called "modern art." And yet, Western artists have been creating abstract* paintings and sculpture for about the last hundred years. It is difficult to think of calling all this art "modern," and yet that is what often happens.

The work of three artists was very important about a century ago. At that time paintings were beginning to look less realistic. These men were Vincent Van Gogh, Paul Gauguin, and Paul Cézanne. They had a great influence on artists who followed them and are often known as the fathers of all the abstract art that has been done since.

Their lives were all very different and you may enjoy reading about them. In this lesson, you will concentrate on the art produced by one of these great artists, Paul Cézanne.

Paul Cezanne (1839 - 1906). *Monte Sainte-Victoire.* Oil on canvas. The Metropolitan Museum of Art. Bequest of Mrs. H.O. Havemeyer. The H.O. Havemeyer Collection.

Paul Cézanne (1839-1906). *Still Life: Apples and a Pot of Primroses.* Oil on canvas. The Metropolitan Museum of Art. Bequest of Samuel A. Lewisohn.

Instructions:

1. Paul Cézanne painted in a very thoughtful way. As he looked at the things around him they all seemed to be made up of geometric shapes* and flat surfaces.* All objects, even very small objects, were painted as though composed of flat planes*. As a result of this kind of analysis, Cézanne's paintings have a distinctive and easily identifiable character. All the planes in his pictures seem to interlock to create complicated geometric jigsaw puzzles.

   Later artists, such as Georges Braque and Pablo Picasso, were influenced strongly by this kind of geometric analysis and used it as the foundation of one of the great schools of art in the 20th century, known as Cubism*.

2. Study as many works of art by Paul Cézanne as you can. Most libraries have art books in which you will find color plates of his paintings. The black and white reproductions shown with this lesson may also help you, although they lack the important quality of Cézanne's use of color.

3. Paint a picture, using any painting medium, of a place or a person you know. The picture is to be entirely your own work; however, it is to be painted with the color range and in the geometric style used by Cézanne. Keep two or more colored reproductions by Cézanne next to you as you work; turn them, or photocopies, in with your painting when it is finished.

4. Submit for evaluation at least two photocopies or reproductions of paintings by Cézanne and a painting of your own using his color range and geometric style.

Learning Outcomes:

1. Describe how Cézanne painted objects in his art work.
2. Explain how the color and style of your painting resembles Cézanne's use of color and style.
3. Paint an original picture in the color range and geometric style used by Cézanne.

16

Suggested Materials:

White paper; pencil and eraser; any paint medium, palette, brushes; water; paper towels

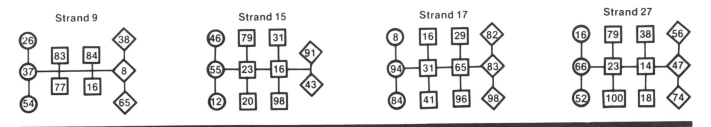

Strand 9

Strand 15

Strand 17

Strand 27

Paul Cézanne (1839-1906). *The Card Players.* Oil on canvas. The Metropolitan Museum of Art. Bequest of Stephen C. Clark.

17

one time printing

Monoprinting is one of the simplest of all surface* printing techniques. "Mono," meaning one, indicates that in monoprinting you make one print only, unlike other printing processes used for books, magazines, and newspapers where many copies are made. Monoprints may be simple enough for kindergarten children to make or sophisticated creations of professional artists. Because every monoprint looks different, possibly one of the most interesting experiences in print making is discovering what a monoprint looks like.

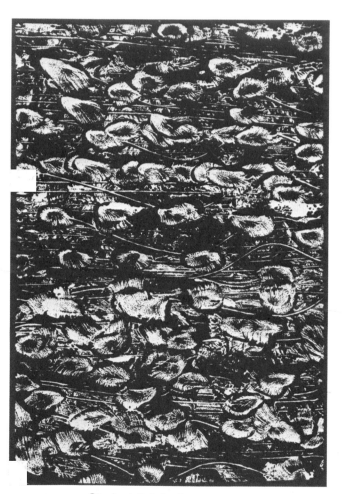

Student finished monoprint.

Instructions:

1. Choose a color of printer's ink and spread it in an even layer on a sheet of glass, with a brayer* or a large paint brush. Experiment by drawing simple lines, shapes, and textures directly into the wet ink with a variety of instruments such as fingers, erasers, scissors, pencils, and razor blades. You may also place natural materials, such as leaves, grass, and feathers on the wet ink surface.

2. Lay a piece of thin white paper on top of your design and rub the entire surface of the paper gently with your hand. Carefully lift the paper from the inked surface. Place it on a table to dry. Make as many "lifts" as the inked design can produce. In additional monoprints, try experimenting with different effects, using the same color ink.

3. Cut out some of the experiments and paste them to a paper surface using rubber cement.

4. Create a final monoprint by repeating some shapes, lines, and textures found in the experiments. Use the same color printer's ink as in your experiments.

5. Submit for evaluation your pasted experiments and the final monoprint composition.

Learning Outcomes:

1. Explain why monoprinting, as a process, produces only one copy.

2. List lines, shapes, and textures in your experimental monoprints that are also found in your final monoprint composition.

3. Choose one color printer's ink to make several experimental monoprints and to create a final monoprint based on these experiments.

Suggested Materials:

Newsprint or other thin paper; pencil and eraser; printer's ink; large paint brush or brayer; water and paper towels; scissors, razor blade, etc.; sponge; glass plate; plastic dinner tray or other flat surface

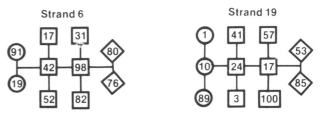

Ron Schemenauer: Courtesy of the artist.

One-color monoprint.

18   sculptural skeletons

When a large building or bridge is constructed, a spider's web of steel girders is erected. Architecture and engineering can thus be thought of as special forms of sculpture. While sculpture does not have to be useful (as architecture does), it should always be good to look at. Also, sculpture does not have to be mammoth-sized or constructed of expensive materials. Creating sculpture that resembles architectural engineering in appearance is possible with inexpensive objects and items that can be found in most places.

Simon Rodia, *Watts Towers* (1921-1954). Los Angeles.
Photo: Julius Schulman.

Instructions:

1. Make a collection of objects that might be useful for building a structure of the kind described, such as sticks, wire, glue, bolts, toothpicks, and parts of discarded toys.

2. Construct a piece of sculpture using a variety of materials from your collection that resembles an architectural skeleton. The result should show a combination of inventive methods of construction and also be pleasing to look at. In addition, the structure should include small and large units that are repeated in different ways. Above all, the structure should be sturdily constructed and show evidence of an appropriate method of attaching materials.

3. Submit for evaluation the skeleton sculpture constructed from a variety of materials.

Learning Outcomes:
1. Describe the method you used to construct your sculpture.
2. Explain ways in which your sculpture is to varying degrees successful or not successful.
3. Construct a sturdy piece of sculpture of a variety of materials to resemble an architectural skeleton.

18

Suggested Materials:
Found objects; suitable materials for attaching the found objects: white (Elmer's) glue, epoxy, "Super" glue, adhesive tape, wire, etc.

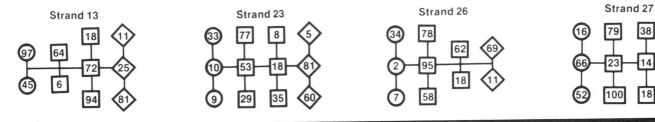

Robert Jacobsen (1912 -). *Le Roi de la Faim.* Museum of Art, Carnegie Institute. Rosenbloom Purchase Fund.

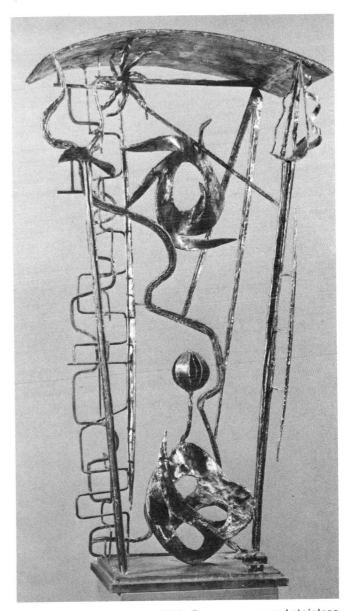

Herbert Ferber. *Sun Wheel* (1956). Brass, copper, and stainless steel. Collection of Whitney Museum of American Art, New York.

19

mosaic art

The art of mosaic requires that designs and pictures be composed of small colored pieces, called tesserae, set side by side to fill a space. Each piece of tesserae touches or nearly touches the piece next to it, but none of the pieces overlap. Most mosaics are made of tesserae that are about the same size and shape. Traditionally, artists from places such as Ancient Rome, Medieval Europe, and contemporary Mexico have used tesserae made from glass and glazed tile to create mosaics. Today, almost anything may be used as long as the mosaic technique described above is followed. For this lesson, you are advised to use light weight materials such as paper and plastic and tin foils.

Instructions:

1. One of the most important concerns for an artist is to convey a message or feeling. In this lesson, you are to decide what message or idea you wish to communicate. Avoid using stereotypical themes such as those that feature Holly Hobby or Snoopy as characters. Should you have trouble finding an idea, you will be able to appreciate better how an artist feels as he or she searches for ideas.

2. On a small piece of paper, sketch your idea in a way that would be appropriate for a mosaic design. Make one shape more outstanding or dominant* and include several other related shapes. In your sketch, indicate how colors will be distributed in the final mosaic. Use one dominant color and at least two other colors. These shapes and colors should enhance the message you wish to convey.

3. Sketch* the overall design for the mosaic on a piece of cardboard not smaller than 9" x 12". Select suitable light weight materials for the tesserae, such as paper, plastics, and tin foils. Cut a quantity of small pieces that you will need. Move the pieces around until the overall silhouette* of your design can be seen. Fill the entire space on your cardboard with tesserae and the spaces between them. Do not overlap tesserae. When your design appears complete, attach the pieces of material with rubber cement to the cardboard.

4. Submit for evaluation the sketch for your mosaic design and your finished 9" x 12", or larger, mosaic.

Student paper mosaic.

Learning Outcomes:

1. Define the words mosaic and tesserac.
2. List the qualities in your mosaic that help convey your message.
3. Make a colored sketch to be used as a basis for a mosaic. Make a 9" x 12", or larger, mosaic from lightweight materials, that conveys a specific message through the use of dominant shapes and colors.

19

Suggested Materials:

Sheet of cardboard, 9" x 12" or larger; drawing paper; crayons for color sketch; scissors; rubber cement; colored paper, metal or plastic foil, buttons, etc.

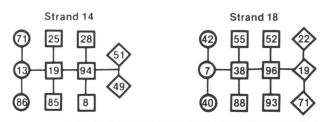

Student paper mosaic.

native american art

Many different native American tribes occupied the United States and Canada before the arrival of Europeans. The art of these peoples reflected the kind of life they lived. Woodlands Native Americans lived differently from those on the prairies, the deserts, the mountainous North West coast, and the low lying swamps of the South East. In this lesson, you will study symbols* found in Native American art from one of these geographic regions, perhaps even from the area in which you live.

Tlingit Tribe, Chief's Chilkat Blanket, (1870-80). Goat wool and cedar bark. Courtesy of the Indiana University Art Museum.

Instructions:

1. Search for information about Native American art. An encyclopedia, or other books you may have on hand, can be helpful. You may have to go to the library to find additional information.

2. Look at the arts and crafts produced by various Native American tribes. Different symbols were used by different tribes to represent objects in the real world that had supernatural powers associated with them. These symbols could represent fertility, life after death, and control over objects in the environment. What meanings do symbols such as the squash blossom, thunderbirds, and bolts of lightening have in different Native American tribes?

3. Choose three symbols used by a specific Native American tribe to study and draw. Each of these three symbols should be drawn, on a separate piece of paper, accurately and large enough to show all details. The symbols can be rendered in pencil, with shading*, to look three dimensional or drawn, with felt tipped pens or India Ink, in a flat, linear* style.

4. For each symbol, write a description of the symbol and its meaning in the particular culture you have chosen to study.

5. Submit for evaluation three separate drawings of symbols from a Native American tribe together with a written description of the meaning of each symbol.

Learning Outcomes:
1. Explain how art from different Native American tribes reflects differences in life styles.
2. Explain why symbols associated with supernatural powers were used by different tribes.
3. Make fairly large drawings of three different symbols; describe meanings to various tribes.

Suggested Materials:
White drawing paper; pencil and eraser; india ink and pen or felt tipped pens; pen and note paper

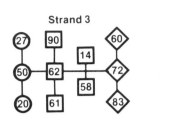

Strand 3

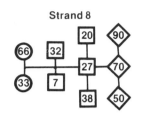

Strand 8

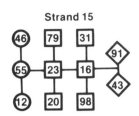

Strand 15

Strand 28

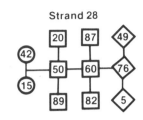

SILVER
NECKLACE
"SQUASH BLOSSOM"
EARLY 1800'S
ARIZONA

Student drawing of native American art.

Woodland - Geometric designs used in loom beading

Woodland - Floral designs used in applique beading

Student drawings of designs based on native American art.

Acoma Pueblo, New Mexico. Jar (late 19th century). Courtesy of the Indianapolis Museum of Art, Julius F. Pratt Fund.

21

Works of art often communicate particular ideas or themes such as "mystery" or "happiness". Artists sometimes choose their own themes. On other occasions, they are given a specific theme and have to create an art work that a purchaser will understand. General themes leave open the possibility of many varied and interesting interpretations. For example, untold thousands of pictures have been painted on the theme of "motherhood." Each has been depicted in a different way yet each expresses the theme of "motherhood."

This lesson is an opportunity to create your own picture based on a theme that other people will understand and yet has specific meaning for you.

Instructions:

1. List five familiar themes that might become sources of interesting pictures. Then list five ideas for pictures based on each theme. For example, three ideas for "happiness" might include a group of happy dancers, a pair of lovers, and a small boy and his dog.

2. When you have decided on a theme that most appeals to you and have written down five ideas for pictures based on that theme, select one of the ideas. Make three small, quick pencil sketches* for a picture based on the best idea for that theme.

3. Select the best sketch and enlarge it to fill a sheet of paper. As you work, modify the picture to make it representational*, or abstract*, or non-objective*. It may be finished as a drawing with full shading* or it may be crayoned or painted — the choice is yours.

4. When finished, write the theme title clearly on the back of the picture.

5. Submit for evaluation the list of five themes and five topics under each theme, three sketches, and the finished picture of the preferred interpretation of the theme.

Three interpretations by artists on the theme of motherhood.

Byzantine, 13th century. Madonna and Child on a Curved Throne. National Gallery of Art. Washington. Andrew W. Mellon Collection.

Learning Outcomes:

1. Explain why artists often base their art ideas on themes.
2. Describe why you chose your interpretation of the theme and not the other ideas you listed.
3. Draw three quick sketch ideas, each illustrating a theme; create a finished picture from one of the sketches in your choice of medium.

21

Suggested Materials:

Paper; pencil and eraser; a preferred medium (pencil, crayons, pastels, paints).

Strand 10

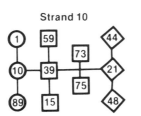

Strand 12

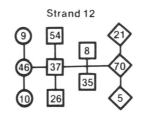

Strand 22

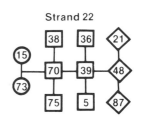

Pablo Picasso (1881-1973). *A Mother Holding a Child and Four Studies of Her Right Hand.* Crayon on paper. Fogg Art Museum, Harvard University. Bequest of Meta and Paul J. Sachs.

Charles White (1918-1979). *Seed of Love* (1969). Ink drawing. Los Angeles County Museum of Art: Museum Purchase, Acquisition Fund.

22   art for advertising

Tissue paper comes in many brilliant colors. When used with diluted white glue to make a collage, the colors become more transparent and brilliant. More startling effects can be achieved if dark opaque* colors are used among the bright, transparent colors. This tissue paper technique will be used, in this lesson, to help you create a record cover for your favorite recording.

Student tissue paper design for a record album cover.

Instructions:

1. Tear or cut a number of similar shapes from tissue paper that are related to the music on one of your favorite recordings. The tissue shapes may overlap or be placed side by side. Arrange these shapes to fill a sheet of white cardboard the size of a record album cover. Use one or two dominant colors and then introduce several other colors that are less dominant.

2. The words you will use on the record album cover are an important part of the design. Make the letters for the words either from dark paper or from words and letters cut from magazines. Make sure the words are easy to read. They should contrast with the background and go with the shapes and colors in the tissue paper design.

3. After you have arranged the words, shapes, and colors in your tissue design so they appear unified, glue the tissue and letters to the cardboard. Dilute white glue with water before it is applied with a brush to cover the tissue paper. Because tissue paper becomes more transparent when saturated with glue, overlapping different colors creates new colors. Overlapping the same or similar colors intensifies the brilliance of colors. Remember all parts of the design should look as if they belong together.

4. Submit for evaluation a tissue paper design the size of a record album cover that represents the music on your favorite recording.

Learning Outcomes:

1. Explain how tissue paper can be used to create a brilliantly colored design.
2. List the ways that unity* is achieved in your tissue paper design.
3. Make a record album that combines words, shapes, and colors using tissue paper and dark construction paper.

Suggested Materials:

Dark construction paper; colored tissue paper; brush; paper towels; scissors; white glue; water; magazines

22

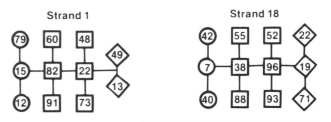

Strand 1

⑦⑨ [60] [48] ◇49◇
⑮—[82]—[22]—◇13◇
⑫ [91] [73]

Strand 18

㊷ [55] [52] ◇22◇
⑦—[38]—[96]—◇19◇
㊵ [88] [93] ◇71◇

Student tissue paper design for a record album cover.

In western culture, working with a needle and thread has traditionally been thought of as something that only women do. This is no longer true. Today, both men and women express themselves using stitchery as an art form. Stitchery art opens new possibilities for your own art work that you may not have previously considered. In this lesson, you will use yarn, sewn on a wire screen, to create a stitchery design.

Instructions:

1. On a sheet of drawing paper, plan a design that can be executed in a yarn stitchery. It may be geometric* or it may depict objects from nature. The design should not be symmetrical*. Indicate the colors in your plan that you intend to use in the finished yarn stitchery. Be sure that the shapes and colors you have chosen go well together and create a unified* design.

2. Take a piece of wire screen that measures at least 12" square. The holes in the screen should be just large enough to allow your yarn to pass through easily. Tape the sharp ends of the screen to strips of cardboard. This will also make a frame for your work.

Thread a needle with yarn. Knot one end to prevent it from pulling through the screen. Begin at the back. Pull the yarn across the front of the screen until you reach a point where you want to stop the line. Then pass the needle and yarn through the screen. Bring it back through the screen to make another line. Continue the process with different yarns and threads until you have created a design that you think is pleasing. Always keep the yarn pulled fairly tight. Cover the entire screen with yarn. Study the illustration to see how to make and use the screen.

3. Submit for evaluation the plan for the yarn stitchery and the finished 12" yarn stitchery.

Leah Orr, *Catalyst* (detail): Courtesy of the artist.   Photo: Bob Wallace.

Learning Outcomes:
1. Explain some of the possibilities that stitchery offers as an art form today.
2. Describe the technique of creating yarn stitchery on a wire screen.
3. Create an asymmetrical 12" square yarn stitchery design on a wire screen, based on a plan that coordinates colors and shapes.

Suggested Materials:

Strips of cardboard; needle; adhesive tape; yarns of various colors and thicknesses; wire screen, 12" square or larger

Strand 5
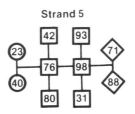

Strand 15
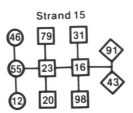

Strand 27
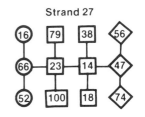

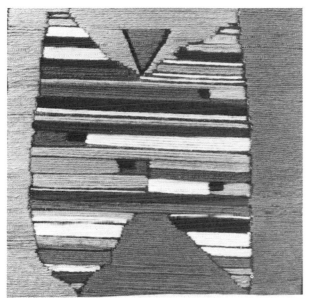

Student yarn stitchery.

Student yarn stitchery.

Yarn stitchery in progress.

Our facial expressions often show how we feel. Another means of communicating feelings and emotions is through what has been described as "body language." Think about various body positions you have observed, without seeing a person's face, and try to remember what these positions have communicated to you. For example, a student slumped at his or her desk, a striker standing with a raised fist, or a soloist involved in playing a musical instrument all convey different feelings and emotions through their body positions.

This lesson asks you to translate your observations of a person in a particular position into a visually expressive statement that conveys a powerful feeling or emotion.

Instructions:

1. Find someone to pose for you or observe a person engaged in an activity that communicates a strong feeling or emotion. The person's whole body should be involved in that activity. Make a full-length sketch* of the person. First, sketch the outline of the body and check for accurate proportions* and correct angles of arms and legs so that the person's posture clearly communicates a message. See page 223 for a checklist of body proportions.

2. Make a finished drawing, based on your sketch, that includes shading* and as many details as you need in order to describe the pose accurately. Label the emotion the feeling conveys on the back of the drawing.

3. Submit for evaluation a full length sketch of a person engaged in an activity that clearly communicates a strong feeling or emotion and a final drawing, based on this sketch, with a label that describes the feeling conveyed.

Auguste Rodin (1840-1917). *St. John the Baptist Preaching.* Pen and ink. Fogg Art Museum, Harvard University. Bequest of Grenville L. Winthrop.

Learning Outcomes:
1. Explain how body positions convey particular feelings and emotions.
2. Describe the feeling or emotion communicated by the pose you have drawn.
3. Make a correctly proportioned, shaded, detailed drawing of an active person which communicates a feeling or emotion.

Suggested Materials:
White drawing paper; drawing pencils and eraser

24

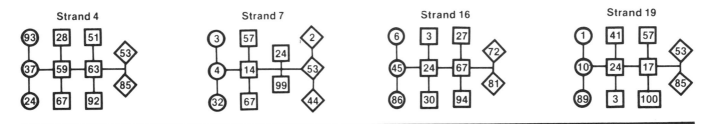

Honoré Daumier (1808-1879). *Connoisseurs.* Watercolor, charcoal, pen and ink. The Cleveland Museum of Art, Purchase, Dudley P. Allen Fund.

57

25   dominance in sculpture

The word "dominance" applied to three dimensional sculptural works has a somewhat different meaning from its use with two dimensional pictorial art. When seen from the front, the dominant* part of a piece of figure sculpture may be the face. When the sculpture is seen from the side, the dominant part may be a hand holding a sword. When seen from the rear, dominance may be found in a shield slung over one shoulder. This piece of sculpture would, therefore, exhibit three instances of dominance depending on the position of the viewers.

In this lesson you will deal with the problem of dominance in sculpture through creating your own piece of sculpture.

Henry Moore. *Family Group* (1948-49). Bronze. Collection, The Museum of Modern Art, New York. A. Conger Goodyear Fund.

Instructions:

1. Sculpture is created by one of two general methods. One is achieved by joining pieces together, the additive* method. The other is achieved by removing pieces, the subtractive* method. While both methods may be used in any single piece, one will usually take precedence over the other. You are to choose one of these methods in your work for this lesson.

2. Another choice to be made is that of subject matter.* Sometimes the choice is set by the client, but just as often it is the artist's own decision. Deciding on your own topic is difficult; it is much easier to be told what to do. In this lesson, you are to make a personal decision about the choice of subject matter.

The only conditions you have to meet are that your sculpture be at least 12" high, that it be made mainly by means of either the additive or subtractive method, and that it show clear evidences of dominance as described in the introduction to this lesson.

4. Submit for evaluation your piece of sculpture in your choice of theme and medium.*

58

Learning Outcomes:

1. Explain how you used the additive or the subtractive method to create your sculpture.
2. Describe how the subject matter, the presence of dominance, the method, and the medium all work together in your sculpture.
3. Create a 12" high piece of additive or subtractive sculpture, in your choice of theme and medium, in which special attention was given to dominance.

25

Suggested Materials:

A suitable sculptural material: clay, plaster, wood, heavy wire, etc.; tools for use with a given material: clay modeling tools; knife for carving clay or plaster, hammer, nails and glue for joining wood, pliers for use with wire, etc.

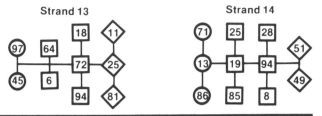

Sung Dynasty, China (960-1280). Head of Kwan Yin, Wood. Worcester Art Museum, MA.

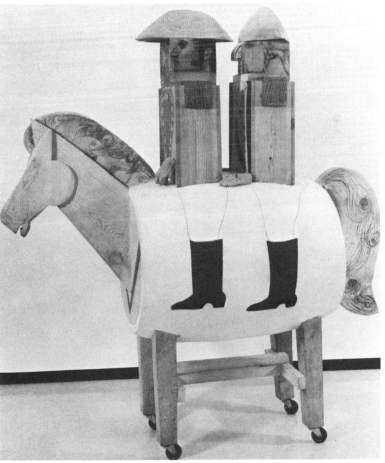

Marisol (Escobar). *The Generals.* Wood and mixed media. Albright-Knox Art Gallery, Buffalo, New York. Gift of Seymour H. Knox.

fade out

On a foggy morning, or just before you go to sleep, or when you squint your eyes, or when you sit and daydream, colors just seem to fade away. In the out of doors, dark colors, that are farther away, appear to be much lighter than they really are whereas light colors appear to be slightly darker. Colors also appear to lose their brilliance as they recede into the distance. Objects in the far distance appear as light to middle gray colors.

These colors appear to be bluish, yellowish, or purplish depending on the color of the sky and the amount of dust in the air. This lesson involves using color perspective to paint an outdoor scene. Smoggy factory scenes, sundrenched orchards, and mountain vistas many times are painted so that colors fade away completely in the distance into haze or fog.

J.M.W. Turner (1775-1851). *The Dogana and Santa Maria della Salute, Venice.* National Gallery of Art, Washington. Gift of Mr. C.V.S. Roosevelt.

Instructions:

1. Select one hue (color). On a sheet of white paper, practice mixing varying amounts of the color and its complement. Complementary colors are those colors that are opposite on the color wheel. For example, red is opposite green, blue is opposite orange, and violet is opposite yellow. When placed side by side these colors contrast strongly, but when they are mixed together, they become dull gray colors.
2. Practice mixing white with your color to make tints* of that color and black to make shades.*

3. In pencil, plan an outdoor scene that shows distance. Include a foreground*, middleground*, and background* and objects in the scene that will help show distance. See diagram, page 223.
4. Paint the plan of your outdoor scene. Use black, white, as well as complementary color mixed with your original color choice, to show distance.
5. Submit for evaluation your practice sheet of mixed colors and a painting of an outdoor scene that stresses distance and color perspective.

Learning Outcomes:

1. Describe how colors change with distance.
2. Explain why complementary colors are often mixed together in paintings that depict distance.
3. Explain how black and white can change a hue.
4. Paint an outdoor scene with a foreground, middleground, background, and objects depicting distance; use one color and its complement.

Suggested Materials:

White painting paper; pencil and eraser; paints; brushes; mixing tray; paper towels; water

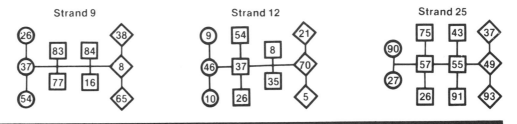

Strand 9   Strand 12   Strand 25

Albert Bierstadt (1830-1902). *Domes of the Yosemite.* Oil on canvas. St. Johnsbury Athenaeum, Vermont.

African art cannot be classified as any one kind of art. In different regions of the African continent, different kinds of art have developed, so that the Moslem art of Egypt, Libya, and Morocco is very different from the tribal art of Nigeria, Ghana, and Zaire. The art of East Africa is also different from art created in West Africa. Art traditions are changing as young African artists are influenced by ideas from other parts of that continent and other parts of the world.

Nevertheless, the art of Africa has its own unique characteristics when compared with the arts of the rest of the world. This lesson is designed to introduce you to African art and to the art of a particular region in Africa.

Student freehand drawing of African art.

Instructions:

1. As you look at African art in books, you may find the art from a particular region more appealing than art from other parts. Also, you may prefer looking at the art of carved wood figures, rather than at pottery, masks, or basket weaving. Alternatively, the design of African building may interest you most of all.

2. When you have arrived at a decision regarding the art forms you prefer and the region in which you believe the art is most pleasing, make careful freehand* drawings of at least three of the most interesting works you can find from that area. Include in your drawings such things as textures, shading*, and as many details as possible that describe the objects. On the back of these drawings, name the region where the object was made, the material it was made from, and its use.

3. Submit for evaluation, three freehand drawings of art works from a particular region in Africa together with information about the objects on the back of the drawing.

Learning Outcomes:

1. Explain why African art is very diverse yet also possesses common characteristics.
2. List the origins, materials, and uses of the objects from Africa you have chosen to draw.
3. Make freehand drawings of three such objects including textures, shading, and details.

27

Suggested Materials:

White drawing paper; pencil and eraser; pen and ink

Strand 3

Strand 8

Strand 16

Strand 25

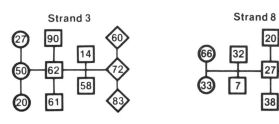

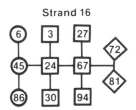

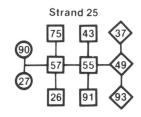

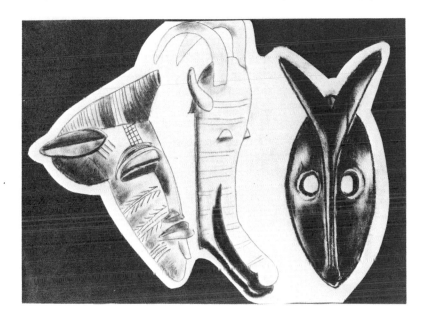

Student freehand drawings of African art.

28 artist as social critic

Historically, artists have been some of the most outspoken critics of society. The Spaniard, Francisco Goya, crucified Spain in his series of prints entitled the "Disasters of War" and his countryman, Pablo Picasso, painted a condemnation of warfare in "Guernica." Käthe Kollwitz, an artist from Germany, also created art depicting the disasters of war during the rise of the Nazis. The Frenchman, Honoré Daumier, poked fun at dishonest lawyers. Jose Orozco, the Mexican muralist, created passionate, patriotic pictures. Today, contemporary political cartoons convey social messages often more succinctly than a thousand words.

The world is full of overwhelming social problems, from urban guerillas, starving people in Asia and Africa, the ecological crisis, to urban decay. This lesson will provide the opportunity to make a visual statement about a contemporary social problem about which you have strong feelings.

Instructions:

1. Choose a contemporary social issue and find a magazine or newspaper headline that focuses on this issue. Collect colored and black and white pictures and words from photographs, magazines, newspapers, and books related to your chosen issue.

2. Make a montage* by fitting the items together to create a forceful visual message about which you have strong feelings. The montage should include a center of interest* around which other images revolve. It should also include the repe-tition of shapes and colors, and an integration of all items with the headline to create a composition* with parts that fit well together. Once you have decided upon the composition of your montage, adhere all items with rubber cement to a 10" x 12" sheet of construction paper or cardboard backing.

3. Submit for evaluation a 10" x 12" montage of magazine and newspaper images that creates a visual statement about a contemporary social problem.

Student montage of a contemporary social issue.

Learning Outcomes:

1. Explain how artists become social critics through visual statements expressed through their art works.

2. Explain the social meaning underlying your montage.

3. List the strengths and weaknesses of the design of your montage.

4. Make a 10'' x 12'' montage about a social issue that incorporates a headline and magazine and newspaper images into a unified composition through use of repetition of shapes and colors and the presence of a center of interest.

28

Suggested Materials:

Cardboard and construction paper; scissors; rubber cement; magazines and newspapers

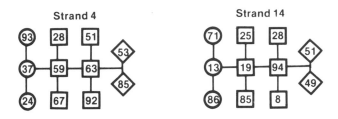

Strand 4

```
(93)  [28]  [51]
                    <53>
(37)  [59]  [63]
                    <85>
(24)  [67]  [92]
```

Strand 14

```
(71)  [25]  [28]
                    <51>
(13)  [19]  [94]
                    <49>
(86)  [85]  [8]
```

Student montage of a contemporary social issue.

women artists

Can you name ten famous women artists? Why are women artists so little known? Due to the recent Women's Liberation Movement, an interest in art work by women has been created. In the past, art made by women was often attributed to male artists who were their contemporaries. It is only during this century that women artists were allowed to study and to show their art work in the same places as male artists. Today, women artists work in a variety of techniques and media and use many different kinds of subject matter in their art work. Professional roles for women artists include architects, sculptors, ceramicists, and painters. You will read about women artists in this lesson and write about two women artists who worked at different times in history.

Mary Cassatt (1845-1926). *The Boating Party.* National Gallery of Art. Washington, Chester Dale Collection.

Instructions:

1. Go to the library and find books about women artists or general art history books. Read about women who painted at different times in history. Names such as Lavina Fontana, Judith Lyster, Rachel Ruych, Angelica Kaufmann, Berthe Marisot, Mary Cassatt, Kathe Kollwitz, Louise Nevelson, and Georgia O'Keeffe should become more familiar to you.

2. Choose a woman artist who worked before 1900 and one who worked after 1900. Write a paper of approximately three pages (1000 words) by responding to the following directives:
   a) Write briefly about the life of each artist and the kind of art work associated with her.
   b) Include a photocopy or reproduction of one work of art representative of each artist.
   c) Briefly describe the media, technique, and subject matter present in each work.
   d) Compare the two art works you have chosen.
   e) Include a reference list of at least three books you have used in your research.

3. Submit for evaluation a three page paper (1000 words) about two women artists, following a specific set of directions, and a photocopy or reproduction of a work by each artist.

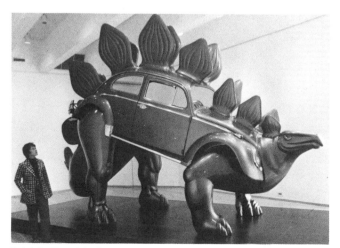

Patricia Rennick. *Stegowagonvolkssaurus.* Steel and fiberglass. Courtesy of the artist. Photo: Laura Chapman.

Artist shown with sculpture.

Learning Outcomes:

1. List the names of ten women artists.
2. Explain why women artists are only recently becoming known to the general public.
3. Write or type a three page paper (1000 words) about two women artists: one who worked before 1900 and one who worked after that date. Answer specific questions about the artists and their art work; include a reference list.

Suggested Materials:

Writing paper; typing paper; pen; typewriter

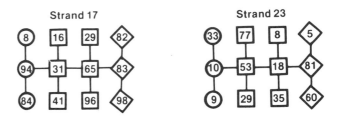

Malvina Hoffman (1887-1966). *Bushman Woman and Baby* (South Africa). Clay. Field Museum of Natural History, Chicago.

You will often want to include images of animals in pictures and designs. But before this can happen you need to learn what various animals look like. One way to do this is by means of careful drawings. Another is to make clay models. In this lesson, you are to draw animals.

Before beginning this lesson you may want to determine whether suitable animals are available to be used as models. While people can be asked to stand still as you draw them and trees do not move very much, animals are unlikely to remain in one position for very long—unless they are stuffed specimens in a museum. You can, of course, restrict yourself to drawing sleeping animals, but that would prevent you from achieving the most benefit from this lesson.

Rajasthan, India (*ca.* 1750). *Raja Riding an Elephant.* Ink drawing. The Cleveland Museum of Art, Purchase, Edward L. Whittemore Fund.

Instructions:

1. Find a large, clear photograph of an animal and draw it carefully. The drawing should be at least 6" in its longest dimension. Avoid animals that have very long hair or those that are fat, since both of these conditions are very difficult to draw successfully.

   The best choice of animal will be one that interests you and about which you already have some knowledge.

   Label the drawing as a study from a photograph.

2. Photographs of animals are unlike real animals: they are flat (or two dimensional*) and not solid (or three dimensional*). For this reason, the next step is to draw a real animal, preferably of the same species as you drew from a photograph. The animal may be alive or part of a museum display.

   Make two drawings of the animal you have chosen from two different, but equally interesting, views. Each view should communicate something different about the animal's appearance.

   Be sure that the general proportions* of the animal are drawn correctly before adding details and shading.* Many animals have interesting markings, but these markings should not obscure the drawing of the solidness of the animal or the texture of its hair or fur.

3. Submit for evaluation one drawing of an animal from a photograph and two drawings of an actual animal.

Learning Outcomes:

1. Explain what you learned about drawing animals.
2. Draw an animal accurately from a photograph.
3. Draw an animal from two different views in correct proportion, clearly showing the solidness of the body, all visible details, and the textures of hair or fur.

Suggested Materials:
Paper; pencil and eraser

30

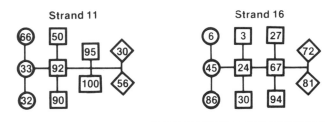

Mughal, Indian (early 17th century). Painting on paper. The Cleveland Museum of Art. Gift of Herbert F. Leisy.

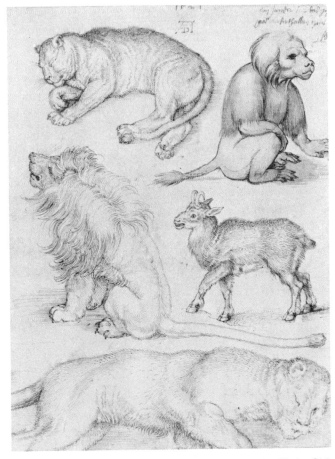

Albrecht Dürer (1471-1528). *Sketches of Animals: Right Side* (detail). Ink drawing with wash. Sterling and Francine Clark Art Institute, Williamstown, Massachusetts.

31 american craftspersons and product designers

During the two hundred years since the United States won its independence, American craftspersons and product designers have risen to international importance and are some of the most respected artists in the world.

In colonial times, craftspersons made useful objects by hand. They made objects such as tools, pottery, furniture, silverware, jewelry, rugs, and quilts. Many contemporary American craftspersons, using hand methods, continue to make similar kinds of objects. From the time of the Industrial Revolution, product designers designed products that were machine made and mass produced rather than objects that were unique and one of a kind. Today, product designers design many of the same kinds of products as craftspersons, but their objects are machine made not hand made. Examples are telephones, computers, airplanes, and automobiles. This lesson is designed to help you find out more about one kind of art product that interests you by tracing its history from the past to the present.

Instructions:

1. Choose a product that has been made and designed in America. Examples would be chairs, tools, telephones, quilts, and automobiles. Find out all you can about the craftspersons and/or designers, past and present, who have been involved in making and designing this product. Trace the history of this product from its early beginnings to present times. Collect photocopies and reproductions or make drawings of the best examples of the work of craftspersons and/or product designers who have been involved in the creation of your chosen product.

2. Write a paper about the product and the craftspersons and product designers who worked on it. The paper should be 1,000 words in length and contain either drawn or xeroxed illustrations. The pictures you have collected should be trimmed and pasted in spaces beside what you have written. Include a reference list of at least three books you have used in your research.

3. Submit for evaluation a written and illustrated paper about the history of a product made and designed in America.

Samuel McIntire (1975). Side chair, mahogany. Courtesy, Museum of Fine Arts, Boston. M. and M. Karolik Collection.

A telephone is designed for mass production.

A microcomputer is designed for mass production.

31

Learning Outcomes:

1. Explain the differences between products made by craftspersons and product designers.
2. List some products made by hand methods and some made by machine methods.
3. Write or type an illustrated paper of at least 1,000 words containing at least three references to the history of your chosen product.

Suggested Materials:

Paper; pen; typewriter; photocopies; reproductions or drawings of an art product

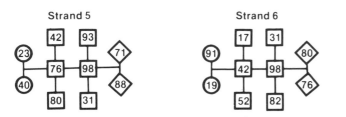
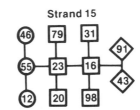
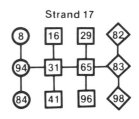

Strand 5   Strand 6   Strand 15   Strand 17

Edward Winslow (1669-1753). Chocolate pot, silver. The Metropolitan Museum of Art. Bequest of A.T. Clearwater.

John Henson. *Bedspread* (1800). Printed cotton and patchwork. Philadelphia Museum of Art. Given by Miss Ella Hodgson (great-granddaughter of John Henson).

This bedspread was designed by John Henson and made by Zibiah Smallwood.

32 how light falls on rounded surfaces

Have you ever tried to draw a ball, a cylinder, or a human body? These shapes have surfaces* that are concave* or convex*, that is, their surfaces are rounded rather than flat. When light hits a convex surface two effects result: the part closest to the light is bright, while the part farthest from the light is dark. Unlike a flat-sided object where shading* changes sharply from one angle to another, on a rounded surface shading changes gradually. However, shading occurs quickly on a sharp curve and gradually on a large slow curve. In this lesson, you will draw a group of rounded objects to help you understand how light falls on these kinds of surfaces.

Instructions:

1. Arrange a group of objects in front of you, all of which have rounded surfaces. Large shapes are easier to draw than small ones. Make sure the light illuminating the objects is mainly from one source so that the gradation* from light to dark on the curved surfaces can be seen easily. A room lit by a flourescent light, for example, is not well suited for this exercise since the light spreads over the entire room and few shadows occur. A single light or lamp bulb is much better.

2. Draw the group of objects to fill a 9" x 12" sheet of paper. Show clearly, in your drawing, what happens when rounded objects are lit by a single source. Use dark and light values* to indicate shading. Include all shadows, especially those that occur under objects and those that fall on other objects. Be sure to show how objects overlap and include all the details you can see. Also, show the difference in appearance between slow and rapid curves. Remember, flat surfaces and the edges that separate them tend to give a feeling of harshness while rounded surfaces tend to suggest gentleness.

3. Submit for evaluation a 9" x 12" drawing of objects with rounded surfaces.

Student drawing of objects with rounded surfaces.

32

Learning Outcomes:

1. Describe what happens when light falls on rounded surfaces.
2. Explain the differences between light falling on a flat surface compared with a round surface.
3. On a 9" x 12" paper, draw a group of round objects, lit from a single source, including shading, shadows, overlapping, and details.

Suggested Materials:

White drawing paper; pencil; pen and ink; black felt pen; black crayon

Strand 7

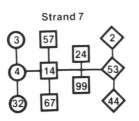

Strand 8

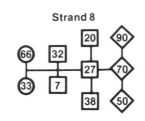

Strand 11

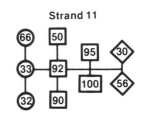

Student drawings of objects with rounded surfaces.

33

small world

Have you ever looked through a microscope? Details that you could not normally see become clearly visible. Even without a microscope the human eye often takes a long time to notice rather obvious details of an object. This is because we are so accustomed to looking quickly at objects to see what they are that we do not examine details of objects carefully. We are usually in too much of a hurry to think of looking intently at

things around us. The purpose of this lesson is to exercise the "microscopic powers" of your eyes by having you examine and draw an object from nature in great detail. One experience of this kind will not make you competent in drawing an object in detail, but it will help you appreciate the wide range of details found in natural objects. Artists often use detail, derived from nature, to create interest and to enhance their art work.

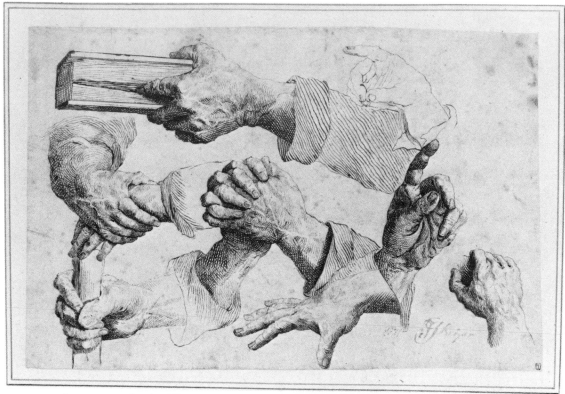

Anonymous. *Study of Ten Hands*. Pen and ink. The National Gallery of Canada, Ottawa.

Instructions:

1. Select an object from nature such as a plant, piece of tree bark, root, a sea shell, a flower, or a leaf. Examine the object for at least ten minutes. If you have access to a magnifying glass, you may use it to discover the very small details of the object. When you think you "know" the object visually, draw it in pencil to fill a sheet of white drawing paper. Make the object look as three dimensional* as possible by including dark and light values* and shadows, although your main task is to show as many details as possible.

2. When you think nothing is left to be added to the drawing, put both the drawing and the object away for a few days. Then, take a fresh look at the object. You will probably discover parts that you had not seen before. Include these newly discovered parts in your drawing.

3. Submit for evaluation the object you drew from nature and the finished detailed pencil drawing of this object.

Learning Outcomes:

1. List reasons why it is important to study an object carefully before making a detailed drawing.
2. Explain why artists use detail in their art work.
3. Make a detailed pencil drawing of a natural object including dark and light values and shadows to create a three dimensional effect.

33

Suggested Materials:

White drawing paper; pencil and eraser; magnifying glass (optional); an object from nature

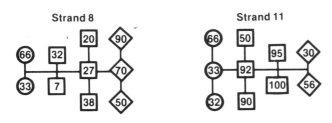

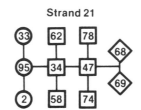

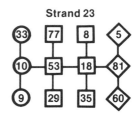

Student detailed pencil drawing of a piece of bark.

Asher B. Durand (1796 - 1886). *Sketch from Nature.* Pencil drawing. The Metropolitan Museum of Art, New York. Bequest of Mrs. John D. Sylvester.

Student detailed pencil drawing of a feather.

34 getting it into perspective

Have you ever looked in a drawing book and seen a mass of straight lines all seeming to be headed for a central point? You probably shut the book quickly and decided that this kind of drawing was not for you. And yet, perspective* drawing is not that difficult and it can help you improve your drawing techniques and skills.

If you look down the middle of a straight street or corridor, everything appears to get smaller, and the lines seem to come together at one point, although you never actually see them meet. This linear* effect is called one point perspective. When you draw this kind of scene, with this kind of perspective, there are a few rules to learn. This lesson will help you learn them so you can draw certain views, such as those down streets and corridors, using one point perspective.

Student one point perspective drawing.

Instructions:

1. Before you choose your scene to draw in one point perspective, try to remember these rules: (a) vertical lines remain vertical, (b) horizontal lines facing you stay horizontal, (c) horizontal lines going away from you, in the direction you are looking, seem to get closer together and converge at one vanishing point. This vanishing point is an imaginary point on the horizon where all receding parallel lines appear to come together. The lines described in (c) slope down if they are above your eye level and slope up if they are below your eye level.

2. Make three fairly quick drawings of indoor or outdoor scenes that show one point perspec-
tive. They should be real scenes you are observing, not imaginary ones. Do not bother with details. Concentrate on making sure the main lines are drawn correctly. You should maintain one eye level so horizontal lines at your eye level remain horizontal.

3. Make a finished drawing, on white drawing paper, of one of the scenes you drew quickly. All details and lines and angles you can see should be drawn accurately in one point perspective.

4. Submit for evaluation three sketches and the finished drawing of an indoor or outdoor scene drawn in one point perspective.

34

Learning Outcomes:

1. List at least three rules for drawing scenes in one point perspective.
2. Explain how a vanishing point is used in one point perspective drawings.
3. Draw three sketches from real scenes that show one point perspective and make a finished, detailed, accurate drawing based on one of the sketches.

Suggested Materials:

White drawing paper; pencil and eraser; ruler

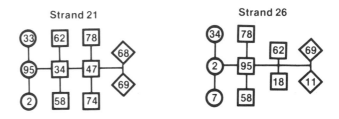

Strand 21

Strand 26

Charles Sheeler (1883-1965). *City Interior.* Painting on board. Worcester Art Museum, Massachusetts.

35 gloomy shadows and flickering light

The art that followed the Renaissance developed into a style* called Baroque*. Many of the great Baroque painters were captivated by dramatic pictures that often became more exciting to look at if they showed bright lighting and dark shadows—the type of lighting usually only seen on the stage. In fact, European art from the 16th to the 18th centuries used many theatrical devices.

Artists as different from each other as Tintoretto, El Greco, Rembrandt, de la Tour, and Rubens all worked in this Baroque tradition. In this lesson, you will make a painting using gloomy shadows and flickering light in the Baroque tradition.

Instructions:

1. Find an interesting scene that is illuminated in a dramatic way so that objects appear as if they are spotlighted. Parts of the scene will stand out sharply, while other parts will appear to be in inky darkness. The position of the light source can make a scene look dramatic. If you cannot find a scene that is dramatically illuminated, arrange one of your own, using bright light such as a reading lamp, a high intensity lamp, or a flashlight.

2. Before you begin your own Baroque style painting, look at the work of artists who worked in a Baroque style in library books or in a museum. Study the ways they created dramatic lighting effects.

3. Plan a picture of a dramatically lit scene. Using tempera paint, create a painting based on the plan that emphasizes and exaggerates brilliant lights and rich darks. Bring out the dramatic feeling of dark and light contrast as seen in one or more of the paintings by Baroque artists that you studied.

4. Submit for evaluation a tempera painting of a dramatically lit scene based on the Baroque style of painting.

Student painting of a dramatically lit scene.

Learning Outcomes:

1. Describe characteristics of Baroque painting.
2. List four or more Baroque painters and contemporary artists who work in that style.
3. In the Baroque style, make a tempera painting of a dramatically lit scene emphasizing brilliant lights and rich dark colors.

35

Suggested Materials:

Heavy paper suitable for painting; pencil and eraser; tempera paint; brushes and mixing tray; water; paper towels

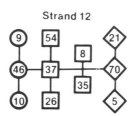

Strand 12

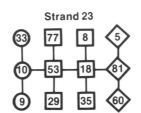

Strand 23

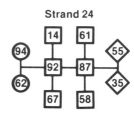

Strand 24

Honoré Daumier (1808-1879). *The Song.* Black chalk, pen and ink, and watercolor. Sterling and Francine Clark Art Institute, Williamstown, Massachusetts.

36

All mentally healthy people enjoy a fantasy life. We regularly daydream while we are "awake" and dream while we are asleep. The real world is unimportant in our fantasies, although the things we fantasize about usually come from what we have actually seen somewhere in real life. Composers write musical fantasies; many stories and poems are fantasies. We see television, movies, plays, operas, and ballets that are often based on fantastic stories. Unreal, romantic, ghostly, mysterious, ideal, grotesque, and playful are a few adjectives that can be used to describe visual fantasy. Some artists depict fantasy scenes that take place in the future on another planet or on the Earth. This type of fantastic art is called science fiction fantasy. If you look at the work of artists who create this type of art it may provide inspiration for creating your own science fiction fantasy art.

M.C. Escher. *Reptiles* (1943). National Gallery of Art, Washington. Rownewald Collection.

Instructions:

1. Relax, dream a little. Imagine you are on another planet at another time. What does the terrain look like? Are there animals and people there? What do they look like? For inspiration, you may want to look in books and magazines for some contemporary science fiction fantasy art work.

2. Make at least two sketches of some ideas for your futuristic fantasy. You may plan closeup views or long range views. Pick the best sketch and use it as a basis for executing a science fiction fantasy scene on a 12" x 14" piece of paper or cardboard. Decide on a medium you think would be most appropriate for depicting your science fiction fantasy scene.

3. Submit for evaluation at least two sketches of a science fiction fantasy scene and a 12" x 14" finished work, based on one of the sketches, executed in a medium* you think is suitable to the choice of topic.

Learning Outcomes:

1. Describe the science fiction fantasy scene you have created.
2. Explain how the medium you chose is appropriate for the scene you have depicted.
3. Create a science fiction fantasy picture that shows either a close-up or a long range view of life on another planet, based on a sketch, and executed in an appropriate medium.

36

Suggested Materials:

Paper or cardboard (at least 12" x 14"); choice of medium such as: paints, oil crayons, wax crayons, colored pencils, pen and ink; scratchboard.

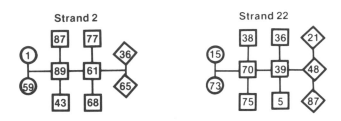

Student finished science fiction fantasies.

focusing attention

People focus their eyes on things that interest them. In much the same way, people focus a camera lens to make sure that the important parts of the picture will be sharp and clear. Artists also paint certain parts of their pictures more clearly than others so that people will look at those parts more than others. If you think consciously about the variations of focus that might be used in your work, it can often result in much more effective picture making.

Instructions:

1. Select either a reproduction of a work of art or a photograph that appeals to you. It should include objects that are near to you, some distance away, and in the far distance. It should also include people somewhere, and their faces should be visible.

2. Make two simple outline drawings of the picture you selected. Each should fill a 12" x 18" sheet of paper.

3. Complete each drawing using paint or a drawing medium* you like to work with. The first one should show only the things close to you clearly in detail (i.e., in focus). Everything else should be progressively more out of focus the farther away the objects are.

   The second drawing should be finished to show only the objects in either the middle distance or the far distance sharply in focus. All the other parts of the picture should be shown progressively more out of focus.

4. Submit for evaluation the reproduction or photograph as well as the two finished pictures, showing different objects in focus.

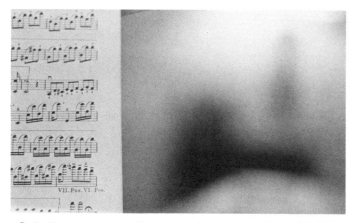

Only the music near the viewer is in sharp focus in this photograph.

Learning Outcomes:

1. Explain why artists choose to focus attention upon certain parts of their pictures.
2. Make two 12'' x 18'' pictures, in your choice of medium; in one, put foreground* objects sharply in focus; in the other, focus on background* or middle distance objects.

37

Suggested Materials:

White paper; pencil and eraser; pen and ink; crayon or felt markers; paints, brushes, palette; water, paper towels

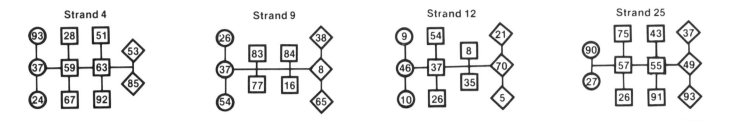

The same photograph with only the cup and saucer, in the middle distance, in sharp focus.

The same photograph with only the lamp and record album, in the far distance, in sharp focus.

38 oriental landscape painting

You may have read that people from the East think differently than people from the West. Historically, that may have been true but changes are rapidly occurring as people all over the world travel and meet. As artists from the East and West see each others' work, their own work is influenced and changed. Eventually, we can expect to see many art ideas developing world-wide and not being confined to particular regions.

Landscape* drawings and paintings are common in both Eastern and Western art. In Japanese and Chinese cultures, landscape drawing and painting has a long tradition. Oriental artists have drawn and painted landscapes to express the oneness of people with nature. They developed special techniques for drawing natural objects such as trees, mountains, rocks, birds, and plants. Many times oriental artists used landscape themes to demonstrate their mastery of drawing and painting techniques. Many Western artists have been influenced by oriental landscape paintings and drawings. In this lesson, you will create your own interpretation of a landscape based on traditional Japanese or Chinese landscape art.

Student interpretation of an oriental landscape.

Instructions:

1. Look in art books and museums for examples of landscape drawings and paintings from Japan and China. Find a landscape drawing or painting that you like. Carefully study it as well as other works by the same artist. Read about the history and meaning of the landscape you have chosen.

2. Create your own landscape drawing or painting based on the one you studied. Do not copy the original, but use similar content*, media*, and techniques* in your work. Try to capture the same mood as the original landscape you have chosen.

3. Photocopy the original drawing or painting. On the back of this photocopy, label the date, country, artist and medium that was used.

4. Submit for evaluation a labeled photocopy of a Japanese or Chinese landscape together with your interpretation, in an appropriate medium*, of the oriental landscape.

Learning Outcomes:

1. List characteristics such as content, technique, and medium found in your art work and in the original landscape drawing or painting.
2. Briefly describe when in history the original was created and something about the life and philosophy of the artist who created it.
3. Create a landscape based on the original.

38

Suggested Materials:

White paper; pencil and eraser; pen and ink; paints; brushes; mixing tray; water, paper towels

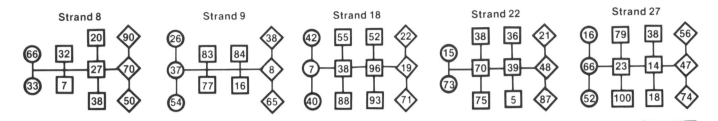

Li Ch'eng (detail).

Li Ch'eng (detail).

Li Ch'eng, Sung Dynasty (ca. 940-967). *Buddhist Temple Amid Clearing Mountain Peaks.* Ink and color on silk. Collection William Rockhill Nelson Gallery of Art, Atkins Museum of Fine Arts, Kansas City.

39

the hidden parts of me

All of us recognize, from time to time, that we are composed of different personalities all wrapped up in a single framework. Consider all the different people we could be in one lifetime and our various dreams, loves, and career hopes. Being a composite of different personalities, we often identify with plants, animals and objects in our environment. Some of us may identify with a cat, lion, log cabin, bridge, willow tree, or rose. This lesson gives you an opportunity to think about yourself and to express visually all the different "yous" within you.

Instructions:

1. Collect various wrapping papers, fabrics, photographs, newspaper clippings, and pictures that contain plants, animals, and objects with which you identify.

2. Cut and arrange your selections of collage materials on a 12" x 18" cardboard to create a visual statement using symbols that together express your whole self. Rubber cement should be used for adhering paper to cardboard. White glue may be used for the fabric and other heavier items. All should be adhered to cardboard to create a collage* that includes various symbols and yet possesses a one-ness or unity* of the total you. To create this unity, you should repeat some symbols*, colors, and shapes. Also, emphasize important symbols by choosing a few that are larger than others, or by having one or two symbols contrast with the others.

3. Submit for evaluation a 12" x 18" collage, with symbols made of various materials, that expresses your inner self.

Marsden Hartley (1877-1943). *Portrait of a German Officer.* Oil on canvas. The Metropolitan Museum of Art, The Alfred Stieglitz Collection.

Learning Outcomes:

1. List the different materials used in your collage and where you located them.
2. Explain how specific symbols contribute to the message of your collage and create a sense of one-ness.
3. Create a 12" x 18" collage that reflects, through the use of symbolism, the different components of your personality.

Suggested Materials:

Pictures from magazines, newspapers, wrapping paper, fabrics, etc.; cardboard; scissors; rubber cement; X-acto knife; white glue

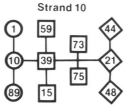

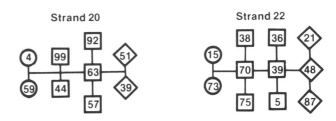

Strand 10   Strand 20   Strand 22

Charles Bird King (1785-1862). *The Vanity of the Artist's Dream.* Oil on canvas. Fogg Art Museum, Harvard University. Gift of Grenville L. Winthrop.

40 painting with stitches

"Painting" with needle and thread can be a unique experience. For centuries skilled artists and craftspersons have used needles and thread to make tapestries and embroideries. Recently, stitchery has become a popular art form as people have discovered that odds and ends of thread or yarn and scraps of fabric can produce attractive and inexpensive works of art.

Stitchery artists use ideas from many cultures as sources for ideas for their designs. They also incorporate different threads, yarns, and cords to add texture and variety to their designs. In this lesson, you will create a stitchery design using a variety of stitches and threads.

Instructions:

1. Using a piece of scrap material, practice making each of the seven sample stitches illustrated in this lesson.

2. When you feel that you can make these stitches, draw a simple line design on a sheet of drawing paper. This is to be the basis of your stitchery "painting." Your design may either be non-objective* or taken from nature. You may look at stitchery designs from different sources for ideas for your design. Do not use commercial kits or copy designs available in commercial kits.

3. Once your line drawing is complete, copy the drawing on a cloth that will serve as a background* color. "Paint" the design with the seven stitches you have practiced using a variety of threads, yarns, and cords and appropriate stitchery to create different shapes and textures. Most shapes can be edged with outline, running, or back stitches. Satin and chain stitches are good fill-ins for larger areas. Select the feather, French knot, and chain stitches for a variety of textures. Combinations create unusual effects, such as the three-dimensional* effect achieved by stitching on top of other stitches. Fill most of the shapes of your design with stitchery.

4. Submit for evaluation the practice fabic with examples of the seven stitches, the line design, and the finished stitchery.

Finished student stitchery.

Learning Outcomes:

1. List the names of the seven stitches used on your practice fabric.
2. Explain how you have used the seven required stitches in your finished stitchery design.
3. Create a stitchery design, either non-objective or derived from nature, that incorporates seven different stitches and has most of the shapes filled with stitchery.

40

Suggested Materials:

For stitching: rug or wool yarn, embroidery floss, raffia, twine, etc.; for background material: duck, poplin, burlap, linen, etc.; for added texture and color: buttons, sequins, metallic fabrics, bark, etc.; tools: darning or tapestry needles, scissors

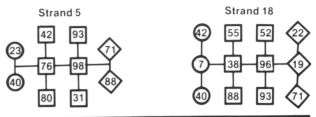

 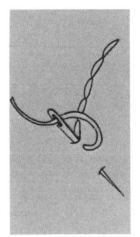 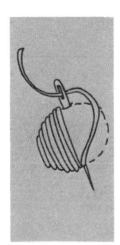 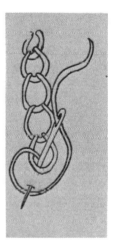

From left to right: Running stitch, Back stitch, Satin stitch, Chain stitch.

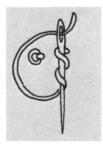 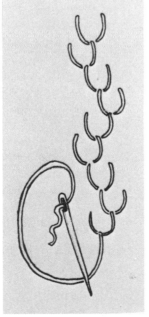

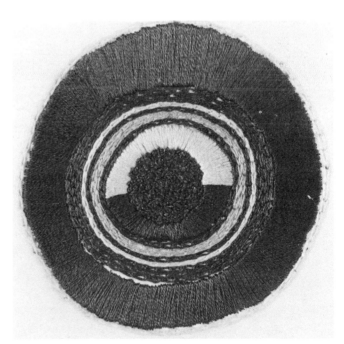

Top left: Outline stitch; top right: Feather stitch; bottom right: French knot.

Finished student stitchery.

41

van gogh

For many people, all painting and sculpture that does not look realistic is called "modern art." And yet, Western artists have been creating abstract* paintings and sculpture for about the last hundred years. It is difficult to think of calling all this art "modern" and yet that is what often happens.

The work of three artists was very important about a century ago. At that time paintings were beginning to look less realistic. These men were Paul Gauguin, Paul Cézanne, and Vincent Van Gogh. They had a great influence on artists who followed them and are often known as the fathers of all the abstract art that has been done since.

Their lives were all very different and you may enjoy reading about them. In this lesson, you will concentrate on the art produced by one of these great artists, Vincent Van Gogh.

Instructions:

1. Vincent Van Gogh was a very passionate man whose pictures are important for the emotions they communicate about people and places. His paintings possess enormous rhythmic power. His brush strokes are repeatedly applied, one next to the other, in a rapid manner so that the emotional feeling of his paintings are further intensified.

   Later artists were influenced by the emotional power expressed in Van Gogh's pictures. His art together with that of Paul Gauguin became one of the foundations for 20th century Expressionism.*

2. Study as many works of art by Vincent Van Gogh as you can. Most libraries have art books in which you will find color plates of his paintings. The black and white pictures shown with this lesson may also help you although they lack the important quality of color.

3. Paint a picture, using any painting medium, of a place or a person you know. The picture is to be entirely your own work; however, it is to be painted with the color range and in the emotional style of Van Gogh. Keep two or more color reproductions by Van Gogh next to you as you work; turn them, or photocopies, in with your own painting when it is finished.

4. Submit for evaluation at least two photocopies or reproductions of paintings by Van Gogh and a painting of your own using his color range and emotional style.

Vincent Van Gogh (1853-1890). *Sunflowers.* Oil on canvas. Philadelphia Museum of Art, The Mr. and Mrs. Carroll S. Tyson Collection.

Learning Outcomes:

1. Describe how Van Gogh communicated his artistic message through the way in which he painted.
2. Explain how the color and emotional style of your painting resembles Van Gogh's use of color and emotion.
3. Paint an original picture in the style used by Van Gogh.

Suggested Materials:

White paper; pencil and eraser; any paint medium, palette, brushes; water; paper towels

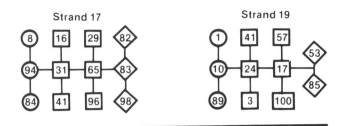

Vincent Van Gogh (1853-1890). *The Starry Night*. Oil on canvas. The Museum of Modern Art, New York. Acquired through the Lillie P. Bliss Bequest.

42

design repetition

The result of repeating a single design unit in a systematic way is called a pattern. Some of the more obvious patterns in everyday life are found in fabrics produced by either a stamped or woven process. Professional designers often use stamp printing methods as they search for new textile, wrapping paper, or wall paper designs.

In this lesson, you will create a repeated design on a sheet of paper using the stamp printing method. This method requires that you carve a simple design unit and print it in an organized way to fill a sheet of paper.

Instructions:

1. Slice a root vegetable, such as a carrot, potato, or turnip, or use a rubber eraser to make the surface* of a stamp. The sliced surface must be perfectly flat. Cut into the flat surface with a sharp knife to create a design. Only the parts of the original flat surface will form the printed image. Practice making a print with your stamp on a piece of newsprint paper. Paint the surface of the stamp with printer's ink or fairly thick tempera paint. To ensure a good quality print, place a smooth, thick pad of newsprint underneath and carefully but firmly stamp the paper. If the stamp does not look right you may alter it. Remember when the design on the block is printed the image is reversed.

2. Experiment with various arrangements of repeats of your stamp to see how the design may be built into larger patterns. Pay as much attention to the blank spaces between the stamp print design as to the design itself. Practice making clear, solid prints with your block.

3. Mark a sheet of newsprint or other fairly thin paper into a grid* with a pencil and ruler. Make sure the size of the individual parts of the grid correspond exactly with the size of your stamp. Then, carefully print all divisions of the grid with a repeated one color stamp print design.

4. Next, print two different repeated stamp designs using the grid format as a guide. These two prints should be two color repeated stamp designs. In addition, you may alter your stamp by cutting portions away. These designs should be neatly and evenly printed.

5. Submit for evaluation the one one-color and the two two-color repeated stamp prints in a grid design format.

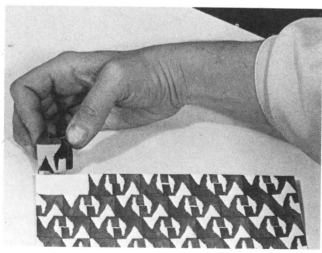

A repeated stamp print in a grid format.

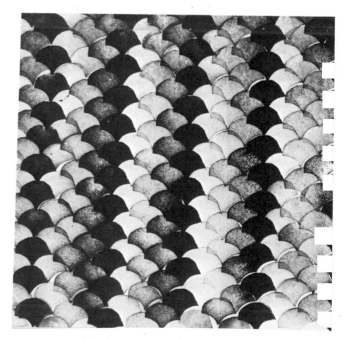

Student repeated stamp prints.

Learning Outcomes:

1. Explain how to make a stamp, to be used for printing, from a vegetable or rubber eraser.
2. Describe how repeated patterns can be made using a stamp print design.
3. Make a one color and two two-color repeated stamp print designs using grids as guides.

42

Suggested Materials:

Thin white paper (i.e. newsprint); pencil and eraser; ruler; tempera paint, brush, water supply; knife; root vegetable: carrot, potato, turnip

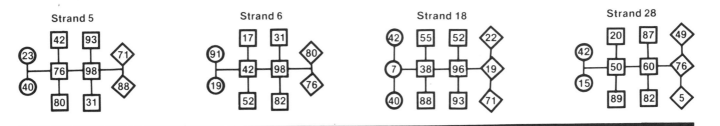

Student repeated stamp prints.

43   landscape abstraction

Western landscape* painting existed in the days of ancient Greece. It was not until the 16th century that landscape painting became popular again. At this time, the painter's skill in recording a scene became important. In the 17th century, Dutch artists painted simple scenes based on real places and the French artist, Claude Lorrain, painted scenes depicting the beauty and grandeur of nature. More recently, artists who paint landscape scenes have bent parts of shapes and stretched other parts until the landscape no longer looks realistic. Artists such as Cézanne, Van Gogh, and Gauguin used landscapes to study the basic structure of shapes, show emotionality through distortion, and create contrasting flat patterns. By changing colors, using geometric shapes, and simplifying the original landscape objects, they made pictures that were termed abstract.

Instructions:

1. Find a photograph of a landscape in a book or magazine. On a sheet of white drawing paper, draw the landscape as accurately as possible. Use a full range of dark and light values. Include all shading and details. See diagram, page 223.

2. Referring to the accurate drawing, on a second piece of drawing paper, simplify each of the large parts into shaded*, patterned*, or dark and light areas. You may make changes from your first, accurate drawing to stress these aspects.

3. Using another sheet of paper, refer now to the second drawing; abstract* each area into a distinct outlined shape. You may make geometric* or free form* shapes. Use a range of darks and lights to fill in the outlined shapes. Fill the shapes with even values; do not use shading.

4. Submit for evaluation a photograph or photocopy of a landscape and an accurate drawing, a simplified drawing, and an abstract drawing based on the original photograph.

Student simplified landscapes.

Learning Outcomes:

1. List several differences between 16th and 17th century landscape paintings and more recent landscape painting.
2. How did you create your abstract landscape?
3. Make three drawings: first, an accurate landscape, then a simplified drawing, and finally an abstract.

Suggested Materials:

White drawing paper; pencil and eraser; pen and ink; felt tipped pen

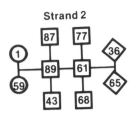

Strand 2

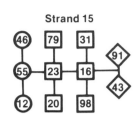

Strand 15

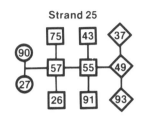

Strand 25

André Derain (1880-1954). *The Old Bridge.* Oil on canvas. National Gallery of Art. Chester Dale Collection.

44   facial expression

We are all creatures of moods and emotions. Often we display emotions such as happiness, sadness, determination, and anger. These feelings are quite often communicated to others much more strongly through facial expressions than through words. Try to remember how you have reacted at different times to being introduced to a celebrity, having someone step on your toe, or hearing unexpected good news. In this lesson, you will have the opportunity to make a drawing of yourself that shows a particular facial expression.

Instructions:

1. Stand in front of a mirror and imagine yourself reacting facially to a number of situations you have experienced. Observe changes in your features as your emotions change.

2. Make a fairly large drawing of yourself showing a particular facial expression such as anger, sadness, or happiness. Draw the portrait as accurately and realistically as you can. Show all lines as you see them. Check that your eyes, nose, mouth, and other features are all drawn in proper proportion.* Include shading* that emphasizes the roundness of parts of the face and also the flat facial planes. Also, include all shadows and details that may help dramatize the emotion you wish to convey. See page 223 for a checklist of facial proportions.

3. Submit for evaluation a drawing of yourself that conveys a particular emotion through facial expression.

Student drawings showing similar facial expressions.

Learning Outcomes:

1. List some emotional reactions you have had to specific situations.
2. Explain how you have used line, shading, shadows, and detail to convey a particular emotion through facial expression.
3. Make a realistic self portrait depicting a particular facial expression.

44

Suggested Materials:

White drawing paper; pencil and eraser

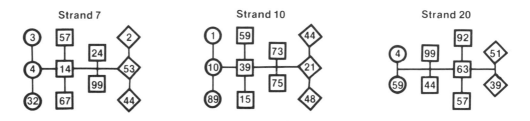

Strand 7

Strand 10

Strand 20

Student drawing showing a contrasting facial expression.

45   handwarming sculpture

Plaster of Paris is a white powder which when mixed with water rapidly hardens. As the liquid turns solid it generates warmth. After it has hardened, it cools and is moist to the touch. When perfectly dry it feels warm and the surface feels hard and chalky.

One of the best ways to develop a feeling for the qualities of plaster is to handle it yourself throughout the various stages of the change from a powder to a solid. This lesson requires you to learn about the qualities of plaster while at the same time using it to create a pleasing looking object.

Instructions:

1. Mix a small quantity of plaster in a bowl. Put water into a bowl and sprinkle plaster into the water until it begins to show through the surface of the water. Then, mix the plaster and water together. As soon as the mixture has begun to thicken, take a handful and hold it between both hands. Hold your fingers slightly apart to allow the plaster to ooze between them.

2. Hold your hands perfectly still until the plaster has become quite hard. The work will be ruined if you move. Notice the speed with which the plaster hardens and the amount of warmth given off during this process of hardening.

2. When the hardening process is completely finished, gently open your hands. Place the plaster piece on one side to dry out thoroughly. Surplus powder and scraps of solid plaster should be carefully collected and deposited in the trash; it should never be flushed down the sink.

3. The plaster block is perfectly dry when it feels slightly warm to the touch and has a slightly hollow ring when gently tapped. This will take several days. At that time, study your piece carefully from all angles. Decide which way it should stand. If necessary, carve a base with a knife so it will stand upright easily.

   Alternatively, you may want to transform the plaster completely by means of carving. The squeezed form then becomes a starting point for your creativity.

4. You may also want to decorate some or all of the surfaces*. Felt markers or paint can be used to add interesting designs. A coating of Elmer's glue should be applied first to prevent the color from being absorbed.

   Designs may also be cut or scratched into the surface.

5. Submit for evaluation a handsized piece of plaster sculpture.

Student hand molded plaster sculptures.

Learning Outcomes:

1. Explain the stages through which plaster goes before it becomes permanently hard.
2. Describe the actions you took to make the sculpture aesthetically pleasing.
3. Make a piece of plaster sculpture by molding it in your hands; modify by carving and/or decoration.

Suggested Materials:

Felt markers; white (Elmer's) glue; paper towels; kitchen knife; bowl; Plaster of Paris; water; newspapers

45

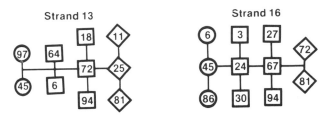

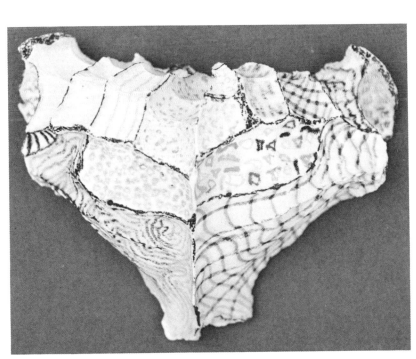

Student hand molded plaster sculpture.

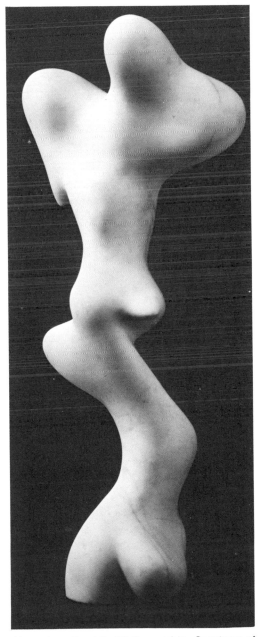

Hans Arp. *Growth.* White marble. Courtesy of The Art Institute of Chicago.

46   a geometric tempera painting

Tempera paint is a water based paint medium used both by young and adult artists. It is inexpensive, mixes easily, and dries quickly. Because tempera is water based it is easy to clean up. Tempera can be applied as thinly or thickly as needed. Smooth and rough textures can be created by mixing different amounts of water with the tempera paint. Your assignment for this lesson is to make a painting which emphasizes smooth application of tempera paint in a geometric design.

An example of 16 student tempera experiments.

Student's finished painted geometric design.

Instructions:

1. Practice mixing tempera paint using a commercial mixing tray or a white glass plate. The tempera paint you use in this lesson should be the consistency of heavy cream. Mix colors (hues) such as red and yellow together to make orange; add white or black to various hues to create tints* and shades*.

2. Divide a sheet of 10'' x 12'' heavy white paper into 16 equal sections. Within the 16 sections paint four circles, four squares, four rectangles, and four triangles with different mixed colors. Use a compass and ruler to form these geometric shapes. Apply the tempera paint evenly. Study the illustration of an example of this sheet.

3. On a heavy sheet of white paper, plan a non-objective* geometric design in pencil that consists of related large and small shapes. Paint one dominant* hue with tints and shades of that hue in your design. Also use small amounts of one or two other colors to create interest and contrast. Work slowly to make a design with straight edges and carefully rounded curves. Apply paint evenly and cover the entire paper, or most of the paper, with geometric shapes.

4. Submit for evaluation the 10'' x 12'' sheet of 16 tempera experiments and the finished tempera painted geometric design.

46

Learning Outcomes:

1. Explain how you mixed tempera paint to create colors, tints, and shades of colors.
2. List at least 5 characteristics of tempera paint.
3. Paint a non-objective geometric design, with tempera of large and small shapes; use a dominant hue, tints and shades of the hue, and small amounts of one or two other colors.

Suggested Materials:

10'' x 12'' heavy white paper; pencil and eraser; tempera paint; small and large pointed brushes; mixing tray or white glass plate; water container and paper towels; compass; ruler

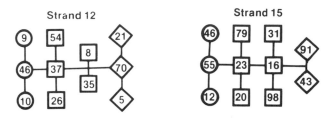

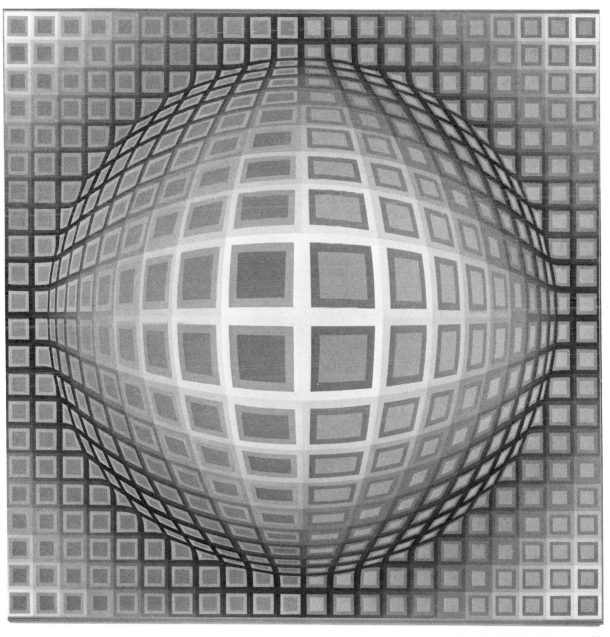

Victor Vasarely (1908 -). *Vega - Nor.* Oil on canvas. Albright-Knox Art Gallery, Buffalo, New York. Gift of Seymour H. Knox.

47 large manufactured objects

Large tractors and semi-trailers are present everywhere. Many are handsome pieces of machinery and have inspired some contemporary artists. Other visually interesting large moving objects include giant coal excavators, sea going freighters, railroad locomotives, road construction machines, army tanks, and aircraft. Bridges and cranes, in contrast, can be equally dramatic but are less mobile.

Large objects can be a source of inspiration for your own art work. In order to draw them, you first have to understand how they work. In this lesson you are to advance your knowledge of one large manufactured object by drawing it.

Instructions:

1. List examples of large equipment of the kind mentioned in the introduction that can be found near your home.
2. Visit one of the objects on your list. You may take a sketchbook and draw the object from different positions or you may fill a roll of film with snapshots. You may also want to study pictures of the machine in books and magazines.
3. Make a detailed drawing of the object using your sketches or snapshots for visual reference. Make sure proportions*, details, shading*, and large and small shapes are correctly drawn.
5. Submit for evaluation the sketches or snapshots and the finished drawings of a large piece of machinery.

Lockheed jetliner (L-1011), courtesy Trans World Airlines.

Learning Outcomes:

1. List pieces of large equipment found near your home.
2. Explain why some artists use large pieces of machinery as themes for their art work.
3. Draw accurately a piece of machinery in great detail.

47

Suggested Materials:

Paper; pencil and eraser; camera (optional)

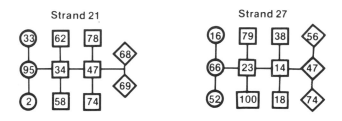

Photograph: Kyu Sun Rhee.

Courtesy: Carnival Cruise Line, Miami, Florida.

48

old age and death

Old age and death are constantly recurring themes in art. Fear, associated with death and dying, shows itself in art across the ages and it is equally present in art works today.

When men and women are young and healthy, they usually live for the excitement of the moment and rarely give much thought to a time when they will be old, perhaps sick, and have to face their own deaths. But growing old happens to everyone; sooner or later everyone dies. If the subject of old age and death is one that motivates you to express your feelings, this lesson offers you an opportunity to do so.

Instructions:

1. Find a poem or an essay that presents old age or death in a way that corresponds with your personal feelings. If you prefer, you may alternatively write a statement of your own that sums up your feelings about death or dying rather than going to some other source.

2. Use the written statement as your inspiration for a visual statement on the same theme. The work may include parts that are realistic or imaginative. Above all you should express your deepest feelings on this most profound topic. You may use any medium* you find appropriate to express your feelings about this theme.

4. Submit for evaluation an art work, in your choice of medium, on the topic of old age and death and a poem or statement about this topic.

Andrew Wyeth. *Beckie King* (1946). Pencil drawing. Dallas Museum of Fine Arts. Gift of Mr. Everett L. DeGolyer.

Learning Outcomes:

1. Describe how the content in your art work relates to a poem or statement about old age and death.
2. Explain why you selected the medium or media as appropriate for your idea.
3. Make an art product inspired by a poem or statement about old age and death.

Suggested Materials:
Your own choice

Strand 1

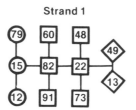

Strand 10

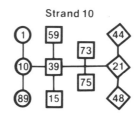

Strand 22

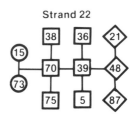

Student drawing on the theme of old age.

Student drawing on the theme of old age and death.

105

49

the persuaders

Advertisements try to persuade people to go to see a new movie, to buy a certain book, to choose a specific brand of shoes, to visit a particular city, or to join the army. These artists select pictures, drawings, and lettering to get their message across to the public so that the design for their product will have more influence on the public than the design for a competing product.

Advertising designs can be glamorous or austere, complex or simple. The only thing that counts is if the design actually persuades people to behave in the manner suggested in the message. Fortunately, the most effective designs also tend to be the best artistically. You have seen countless examples of advertising art; in this lesson you will have the opportunity to design your own.

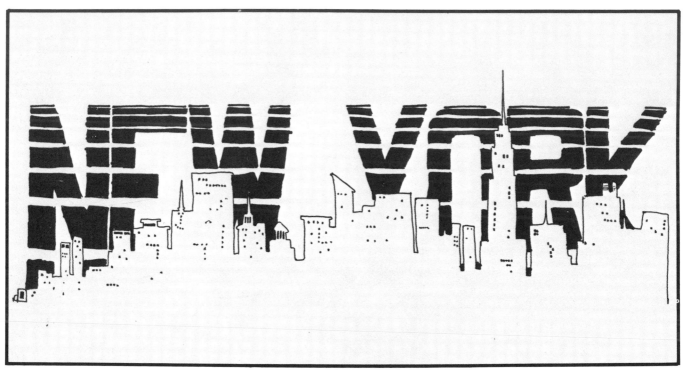

Student pen and ink drawn advertisement.

Instructions:

1. Choose an object or person that represents the product you wish to advertise. You can be advertising a household product, hi-fi equipment, clothes, or a Caribbean vacation. Probably the best choice is something you know a great deal about and especially something you are enthusiastic about.

2. Make the object or person the central theme of your advertisement. Draw or paint a full-sized rendering of your advertisement in the most professional looking way possible. Although advertising artists regularly use photographs and other aids, you are to do everything yourself. You can use any combination of media such as pencils, paints, or crayons. You may cover up spaces and rough edges with white paint.

3. Choose lettering that goes well with your central theme. You may make your own lettering or use stencil* or press type* letters. Use only a few words to describe the product. The words should be easy to read and contrast with the background.* Consider the blank spaces in the background as part of the design. Be sure that lettering and visuals go well together and are well balanced.

4. Submit for evaluation a full-sized advertisement rendered in your choice of media*.

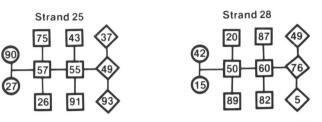

49

Learning Outcomes:
1. Explain how your advertisment is designed to persuade people to do or buy something.
2. Describe how blank background spaces, lettering, and visuals work together to create a unified* design.
3. Design and execute a full-sized advertisement.

Suggested Materials:
Your own choice

Strand 1

79 60 48
15 82 22 49
13
12 91 73

Strand 14

71 25 28
13 19 94 51
49
86 85 8

Strand 25

75 43 37
90 57 55 49
27 93
26 91

Strand 28

20 87 49
42 50 60 76
15 5
89 82

Student painted and drawn advertisement.

Student painted advertisement.

Student collage advertisement.

50 art of pre-columbian america

Before the Spanish invasion of America in the 16th century, great neolithic civilizations flourished for thousands of years in what is now Mexico and Guatemala and in the Northern Andes Mountains in Colombia, Bolivia, and Peru. Different groups came to power and each built great stone cities to worship their gods. At the heart of their religious beliefs was the sun, the source of all things. Gold, the only metal they used, symbolized the sun.

One of the great peoples of these civilizations were the Mayans. Their temple cities were scattered over Mexico and Guatemala. Another people, the Aztecs, were masters of the last great empire in Mexico that was conquered by the army of Hernando Cortes following his invasion in 1519.

The art of pre-Columbian America looks very different from any other art. Pre-Columbian art is an important part of our American artistic heritage and we should become familiar with it.

Instructions:

1. Look at a number of art books that contain reproductions of pre-Columbian art. Fill a sheet of paper with drawings of at least ten different kinds of pre-Columbian art. You may choose objects such as buildings, sculptures, manuscripts, ceramics, murals, and paintings. Be sure to use clear pictures as sources for your drawings. Draw the main shapes and details that make the objects easily identifiable. Check the proportions* against those visible in the photographs. You need not include shading* and shadows. Beside each object, neatly write the name of the object, where it came from, and the people who made it.

2. Submit for evaluation the sheet of ten labeled drawings of pre-Columbian art objects together with photocopies of the original sources you used.

Pre-Columbian Mexico. Page from manuscript *Code Zouche-Nuttal.* Courtesy, The British Museum, London.

50

Learning Outcomes:

1. List several places where great civilizations flourished in North and South America before the Europeans arrived.
2. Discuss how religious beliefs influenced pre-Columbian art.
3. Make and label for identification ten drawings of various kinds of pre-Columbian art.

Suggested Materials:

White drawing paper; pencil and eraser

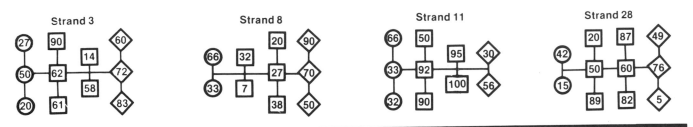

Strand 3 | Strand 8 | Strand 11 | Strand 28

Pre-Columbian Mexico (Teotihuacan). Incense burner. Ceramic. Natural History Museum, Los Angeles. Gift of Dr. and Mrs. Robert Kuhn.

Pre-Columbian Mexico (Guerrero). 15th century figure; carved basaltic rock. Philadelphia Museum of Art. The Louise and Walter Arensberg Collection.

109

51

the public image of a well-known person

Some people are committed to a way of thinking that allows them to be themselves, while others invent public images of themselves. Many people in politics and in the entertainment industry hire publicity agents to dramatize or to enhance their images. These agents suggest mannerisms, dress, speech, philosophies, and even choice of friends.

This lesson gives you an opportunity to describe visually your interpretation of a well-known person's public image. We all "read" people by how they look and by what they say and do. This kind of visual literacy is becoming more important as we see an increasing number of important people on television presentations.

Instructions:

1. Choose a famous person who interests you. You need not admire the person you select. Search books and magazines for photographs of that person in such characteristic poses as walking with associates, working, relaxing with his or her family, or eating.

2. Neatly adhere these photographs with rubber cement to drawing paper. On the same sheet or another sheet of drawing paper, draw the person you have studied in the way his or her personality actually appears to you. You may exaggerate*, distort*, or draw a caricature of the person. Use an appropriate medium* for your drawing such as colored pencil, pen and ink, or felt tipped pens. The quality of the lines you draw will be most important in making the drawing successful. Use a variety of lines such as thick, thin, straight, curved, broken, and continuous lines.

3. Submit for evaluation a sheet of photographs of a well-known person and a drawing of that person.

Student caricature of a well known person.

Learning Outcomes:

1. Explain how photographs of the famous person you selected capture that person's personality.
2. Describe how your drawing communicates your feelings about a well-known person.
3. Using a variety of lines and techniques such as distortion and exaggeration, draw a person so that his or her personality is communicated fully.

Suggested Materials:

Drawing paper; pencil and eraser; pen and ink; colored pencils; felt tipped pens; scissors; rubber cement; magazines and books

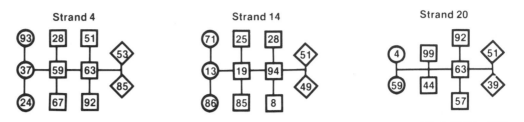

Strand 4

Strand 14

Strand 20

Student collection of photographs of a well known person with a drawing.

52

scratch a picture

The lowly school crayon is really a most versatile drawing tool and is used by many professional artists. If used correctly, crayons can produce beautiful and subtle colors. One purpose of this lesson is to help you realize that most art media* can be used by people of all ages and all levels of talent. The most important goal, however, is to learn to use media to communicate ideas. In this lesson, you will learn a new technique for using crayons called crayon etching.

Instructions:

1. Find a human figure, animal, bird, or insect that contains colors and patterns* appropriate for creating a design stressing color contrast. Make a color sketch* of the animal and a background* that goes with it. Think of colors and patterns that best express your animal.

2. Cover the entire surface of a heavy piece of drawing paper with shapes that contain a number of different crayon colors that relate to the color and patterns of the animal. Avoid using one evenly applied color on your paper. When coloring, press heavily on your crayons so that the finished crayon shapes "shine."

3. Paint over the entire crayoned paper with India ink. Alternatively, but not as effectively, you may use thick black tempera paint instead. Be sure that all the crayoned shapes are covered with ink or tempera paint. When the black cov-ering is perfectly dry, using your sketch as a guide, scratch away parts with the point of a pair of scissors or the point of a nail. Anything with a pointed end will work well. As you remove the black covering, the colors underneath will be revealed. They will look more brilliant than usual because the black will create a strong contrast. Although you should use a variety of lines, do not simply create a line drawing from your sketch. Use the sketch as the foundation for an original composition of lines, shapes, and patterns that go well together. Try all kinds of experiments. If you make a mistake, all you need to do is to paint over the mistake with black and begin again.

4. Submit for evaluation a color sketch of an animal or human figure and a finished crayon etching based on the sketch.

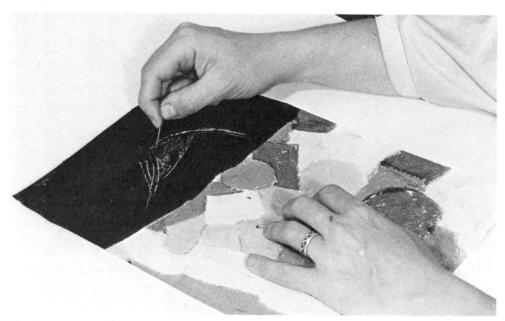

The three steps in making a crayon etching: 1) paper covered with crayoned shapes; 2) inked area covering crayon; 3) inked surface scratched to expose crayon.

112

Learning Outcomes:

1. Explain how color, line, shape, and pattern in the crayon etching are related to the chosen subject.
2. List the processes involved in creating a crayon etching.
3. Make a crayon etching of an animal or person in a way that stresses color contrast, line, shape, and pattern.

52

Suggested Materials:

White paper; black India ink or black tempera paint; brush, water, paper towels; sharp instrument such as a scissors, nail or wire paper clip

Strand 6
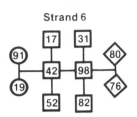

Strand 18
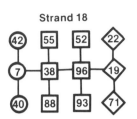

Strand 27
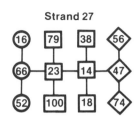

Student crayon etchings.

113

53

mob!

The term "frenzied mob" conjures visions of a turning, twisting, surging mass of people. Mobs usually form when the collective emotions of crowds are whipped into action by persuasive leaders. Artists throughout history have been inspired to portray mobs of people engaged in political or religious frenzy. Often these works have become influential statements about the times in which they were created.

In this lesson, you are asked to convey the fury of a mob. The idea is not to condemn the mob, but to capture its character pictorially.

Instructions:

1. Search for examples of mobs as portrayed in magazines, books, or prints. Your topic could be a political demonstration, a military defeat, or a rock concert. Notice how body angle, gesture, and facial expression communicate emotion. Also, pay attention to overlapping size and group movement.

2. Cut out, trace, or photocopy some of the photographs you have found. Assemble them in position and rubber cement them to a sheet of drawing paper.

3. Use the cut out composition as the basis of a drawing or painting about the frenzy of a mob. The picture will be finished when it communicates the drama of mob behavior through overlapping, size, and group movement as well as with the actions of individuals. Because all the people are experiencing a single driving emotion, the picture should exhibit strong rhythmic movements*. Write the title of your work on the back of the picture.

4. Submit for evaluation the cut-out composition* of the frenzy of a mob and a titled drawing or painting based on the cut-out composition.

Student charcoal drawing of a mob.

114

Learning Outcomes:

1. Explain why artists have been inspired by the theme of a frenzied mob.
2. Explain how the title of your picture fits the emotion expressed in it.
3. Draw or paint a picture of a mob scene depicting emotions through overlapping, size, action, etc.

Suggested Materials:

White drawing paper; pencil and eraser; pen and ink; felt pens; paints, brushes; mixing tray; water, paper towels

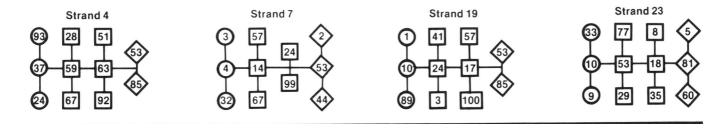

Strand 4 · Strand 7 · Strand 19 · Strand 23

Student pencil drawing of a mob.

"RUMBLE"

Student ink drawing of a mob.

54

so far away

Many painters have been fascinated by the way colors and shapes appear to change as they are viewed in the distance. For centuries, watercolor artists in China and Japan and later in England and America tried to capture the feeling of distance in their paintings. They used darker contrasting colors in closer parts and lighter, muted colors in more distant parts of their pictures. They also showed softer outlines of shapes and less detail in objects in the distance. The illusion of depth created by muting colors and softening of focus of distant objects is called aerial or atmospheric perspective*.

This lesson is an opportunity for you to develop your skill in painting with watercolors. You will use this skill to create a watercolor painting that communicates a feeling of distance.

Instructions:

1. Draw three horizontal lines, about five inches apart, across a sheet of white paper. On this paper, you will make a value chart showing color change in three different colors. You will practice making the lightest to darkest versions of the colors you have chosen. Begin by placing a small amount of one color and a large amount of water on your brush. Wipe the brush and paint a few strokes of pale water color. Let the paint dry. Paint a few strokes next to them with slightly less water. Your color will be a little brighter. Let that dry. Repeat this process until you have reached the brightest your chosen color can be. This is pure color. In this exercise, vary only the amount of water with the color to change it. Do the same with two more colors.

2. The basic rule, whenever you are painting pictures with transparent watercolor is always to begin with the palest colors and move gradually to the darker more intense ones. The darkest colors are the least diluted with water and added last. Do not use white paint in transparent watercolor paintings, white parts of your paper should be used to create white. Black may be mixed with color to create darker colors.

3. On another sheet of watercolor paper, plan a landscape* lightly in pencil. Include a foreground*, middleground*, and background*. See diagram on page 223. Place objects that appear larger in the foreground and those that are smaller in the background. Use muted colors and softer focus of shapes and fewer details for objects in the distance. Use darker, more intense colors for objects that are closer.

4. Submit for evaluation your value chart and your landscape painting.

Winslow Homer (1836-1910). *Homosassa River.* Watercolor. Courtesy of The Brooklyn Museum.

Learning Outcomes:

1. Define aerial or atmospheric perspective.
2. Explain how you created an illusion of distance in your watercolor painting.
3. Paint a value chart using three different transparent watercolors and paint a watercolor landscape using muted color, indistinct shape outlines, and little detail to convey a sense of distance.

54

Suggested Materials:

White paper; pencil and eraser; transparent watercolors, brushes, mixing tray; water, paper towels

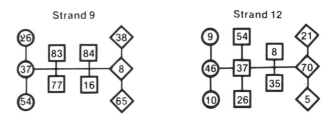

Student painting of a landscape.

Shen Chou (1427-1509). *Peach Blossom Valley.* Watercolor. Courtesy of the British Museum, London.

117

55

stained glass windows

Chartres Cathedral is one of the great masterpieces of French medieval architecture. Its great variety of stained glass windows has been a source of inspiration to many people who have viewed them. Chartres is one of the few medieval cathedrals that still retains most of its original stained glass windows. The kaleidoscope brilliance of the colored segments of Chartres' and other medieval stained glass windows creates a religious feeling as well as telling biblical stories. Many modern stained glass windows use either representational subject matter* or entirely non-objective* designs where the balance of color and line is more important than a story. Both medieval and contemporary stained glass windows are made from glass, ranging from clear, jewel-like transparency to milky translucency; pieces are held in place by lead segments.

This lesson offers you an opportunity to make a design for a stained glass window that is based on the design of one of the great windows executed during the Middle Ages.

Instructions:

1. Look at stained glass windows from the Middle Ages in art history books. The Middle Ages took place in the period of European history between 500 A.D. and 1500 A.D. Find a window that appeals to you. Study the window in detail, paying attention to color, line, shape, and subject matter.

2. Make an original sketch for your own stained glass window. Base your design on the design, or part of the design, of the medieval stained glass window you studied. Create a new design; do not copy the design you used as a source for ideas.

3. Collect various colored, transparent, or translucent materials such as cellophane, acetate, wax paper, and tissue paper.

4. Enlarge the design you sketched for the window on a piece of black cardboard. Cut out the "window" segments with a razor blade or X-acto knife*, leaving holes for the "glass." The "leaded" areas, to give support, should be at least ¼" thick in small designs and ½" thick in large designs. Cut the transparent and translucent materials to fit over the open segments. Rubber cement them on the back side of the cut-out cardboard. Fill all panes with color. The window should be an unusual and attractive design and should be executed neatly.

5. Submit for evaluation a photocopy of the medieval stained glass window that inspired your design, a sketch of the design, and the finished stained glass window design.

Student design for a stained glass window: Cardboard and cellophane.

Learning Outcomes:

1. Explain how your stained glass window is derived from a Middle Ages' design.
2. Describe procedures for creating a design for a stained glass window made from transparent and translucent materials and black cardboard.
3. Using these procedures, design a simulated stained glass window.

Suggested Materials:

Drawing paper; pencil and eraser; thin black cardboard; cellophane, acetate, wax paper, tissue paper, etc.; scissors; rubber cement; razor blade, x-acto or other sharp knife

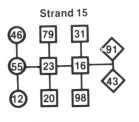

Strand 15

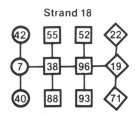

Strand 18

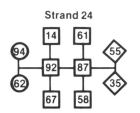

Strand 24

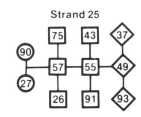

Strand 25

Rose window. York Minister, England (15th century). Photo: Gilbert Clark.

Detail of stained glass window, Austria (*ca.* 1380). The Metropolitan Museum of Art. The Cloisters Collection Purchase.

Student design for a stained glass window: Cardboard and cellophane.

Almost all landscape* art includes trees. For this reason, people who think they might draw or paint landscapes need to be able to draw some of the more common species of trees. The first step in this task is to be able to show the main silhouettes* of one or more of the three main types of trees, namely, conifers, deciduous, and palm. But since silhouettes only show outer contours*, you also need to practice drawing trunks, branches, and foliage.

In this lesson, you are to study a tree, from the area where you live, to the point that you can draw it accurately. In this way you will have practice in drawing a tree that you might include in a future landscape picture.

Instructions:

1. Find a large, clear photograph of a tree and draw it carefully. The drawing should be at least 9" high. Be sure that the general proportions of the tree are shown accurately; add all details and shading* that are visible. Label the drawing as a study from a photograph.

2. Photographs of trees are unlike real trees; they are flat (or two dimensional*) and not solid (or three dimensional*). For this reason, the next step is to draw a real tree. While you may draw a tree you can see through a window the best solution is to go outdoors.

   When preparing to draw outdoors, be sure your paper is firmly attached to a rigid, flat surface. Take extra paper and pencils with you. Select a tree to draw; walk around it to find the best view. Sit as close to the tree as you can without having to move your head to see all of it at one time.

   The drawing should be at least 9" high. First of all, the proportions of the general silhouette should be drawn in quickly and checked for accuracy. Then show the main branches. On most trees the foliage appears as masses of light and dark areas. Show the placement of these masses inside the general silhouette.

   You are now ready to draw in greater detail. Shade the trunk and branches so they look solid. Since you cannot draw every leaf, create textures that represent the various masses of leaves. These leafy masses are three dimensional so parts of them will be lighter than others. Some of the leafy masses that are nearer to you will need to be drawn in greater detail than those that are farther away or in deep shadow.

   In the winter, when deciduous trees are leafless, your attention will focus on the branches. The branches that project toward you will need to be drawn in greater detail and with heavier lines and shading than branches that are farther away from you.

3. Submit for evaluation two 9" drawings of trees, one drawn from a photograph and one drawn from an actual tree.

Cesare da Sesto (1480-1521). *Tree*. Ink drawing. The Royal Library, Windsor Castle. England.

Learning Outcomes:

1. Explain some techniques you learned about drawing trees.
2. Draw a tree accurately from a photograph.
3. Draw a real tree with emphasis on accurate proportions, textures to show foliage, and shading to distinguish parts which are near or far.

Suggested Materials:

Paper; pencil and eraser

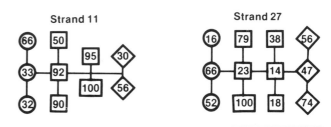

Wen Cheng-Ming (1470-1559). *The Seven Junipers.* Ink drawing. Honolulu Academy of Arts. Gift of Mrs. Carter Galt, 1952.

Most people think that art museums are display areas for paintings and sculpture exclusively. Few consider that drawings usually make up a large part of an art museum's collection. Drawings are created for various purposes and are made with a variety of media and tools. In this lesson, you will be asked to look carefully at and to answer questions about drawings in a museum collection. Looking carefully at drawings will help you become aware of some essential elements in the art of drawing such as subject matter*, linear qualitites, dark and light contrast, and mood.

Instructions:

1. Visit a museum in your community, or nearby, that has a drawing collection. Read the following directions and try to find drawings in the collection that match the directions. For each drawing give the title, the name of the artist, and the date. Do not simply name drawings, give reasons and descriptions in your answers. Keep your answers brief.

(a) Drawings are often used as preparatory sketches for finished paintings, pieces of sculpture, or buildings. Drawings are also made as finished art products and not just preparatory sketches for other art work. Explain why you think one drawing was made as a preparatory sketch and another was made as a finished work of art.

(b) Professional artists use a variety of media* when they draw. They not only draw with pencils, they also use chalks, pastels, charcoal, crayons, and ink. Describe different media that were used to create two different drawings.

(c) Drawings are made from a variety of lines such as thin and thick, short and long, curved and straight, broken and continuous, jerky and smooth, restless and quiet lines. Describe a variety of lines found in two different drawings.

(d) Lines may suggest motion. Different directions of lines — horizontal, vertical, diagonal — combined with different linear quality — short, fast lines or long, heavy lines — can create different movements in a drawing. Describe the movements in a drawing in terms of the dominant direction and quality of lines used.

(e) Some drawings use a variety of gray areas while others use mostly black and white. Drawings may have very subtle contrast of dark and light values*; others use sharp contrast. Describe value contrast used in a specific drawing.

(f) Media, motion, shape, and value contrast along with subject matter in a drawing can create a particular mood. Explain how all these qualities contribute to the mood of a particular drawing that you think is very successful.

2. Submit for evaluation answers to seven sets of questions about drawings in a museum.

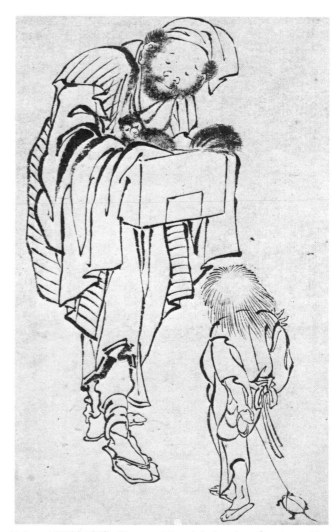

Hokusai (1760-1849). *Man and Boy.* Ink drawing. Courtesy, The Freer Gallery of Art. Smithsonian Institution, Washington, D.C.

Learning Outcomes:

1. List seven classifications used to describe drawings such as linear quality and value contrast.

2. Describe drawings in a museum by writing answers to seven specific sets of questions and directions.

Suggested Materials:

Writing paper; typing paper; paper and pen; typewriter

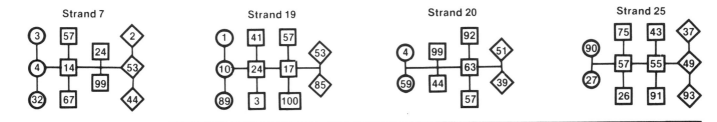

Strand 7   Strand 19   Strand 20   Strand 25

Pierre Auguste Renoir (1841-1919). *The Bathers.* Chalk on paper. Fogg Art Museum, Harvard University. Collection of Maurice Wertheim.

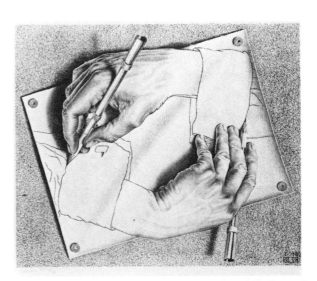

M.C. Escher. *Drawing Hands* (1948). National Gallery of Art. Washington. Rosenwald Collection.

123

renaissance perspective

Since the Italian Renaissance, people have come to expect pictures to be realistic. Part of this happened because of the desire to recapture the Classical* tradition of Greece and Rome. An equally important reason was the discovery of how to draw in perspective*. The Italian architect, Filippo Brunelleschi (1377-1446), developed geometric rules for drawing objects, especially buildings, so that they appeared to look the way people see them.

In this lesson, you will learn the skill of showing objects so they look realistic. The lesson is an introduction to perspective drawing.

Instructions:

1. Find a fairly simple view of a group of flat sided, rectangular objects. It can be an interior of a room or an exterior scene.

2. Hold a piece of plexiglass between you and the scene. Be sure to hold it at right angles to the scene. A sheet of glass is also satisfactory, although sharp edges should be taped. Make sure the plexiglass can be held still while you work.

3. Use crayon or grease pencil and trace on the plexiglass all the main contours* of the objects you can see, especially all straight edges. All objects that are visible through the plexiglass are to be in your picture.

   Study the illustration to see how to make the drawing.

4. When the main lines have been drawn, place the plexiglass on a piece of white paper to make the lines show up clearly. Copy the lines from the plexiglass onto a piece of clean white paper as shown in the illustration.

5. Look at the scene again and add shading* and details to the line drawing on the piece of paper to complete it.

6. Submit for evaluation the plexiglass with lines drawn on it and the finished drawing on paper.

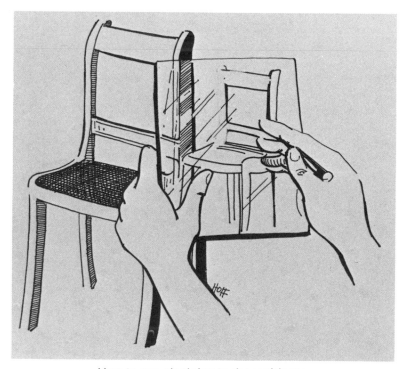

How to use plexiglas to draw objects.

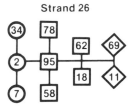

Learning Outcomes:

1. Describe how drawing on plexiglass helped you to do your perspective drawing.
2. Explain why you think people want to see objects drawn realistically.
3. Copy the lines drawn in grease pencil on plexiglass onto a sheet of paper and complete the drawing by adding shading and details.

Suggested Materials:

White paper; pencil and eraser; grease pencil; sheet of clear plexiglass approximately 9" x 12"

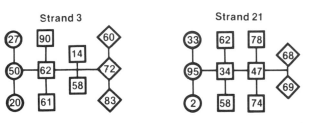

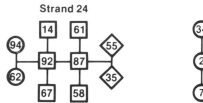

Richard Estes (1936 -). *Drugstore.* Oil on canvas. Courtesy of the Art Institute of Chicago. Edgar Kaufman restricted gift.

a photo-montage mood

Try to think of the number of times you have said, "I'm not in the mood." What kind of mood was it? We all experience different moods; we are excited, relaxed, loving, acting silly, or jealous — to name just a few. The moods people are in can usually be seen in the expressions on their faces.

These expressions change in an instant as the mood changes. This lesson offers you the chance to attend to facial expressions and how they convey a mood by creating a montage* made of cut and pasted photographs.

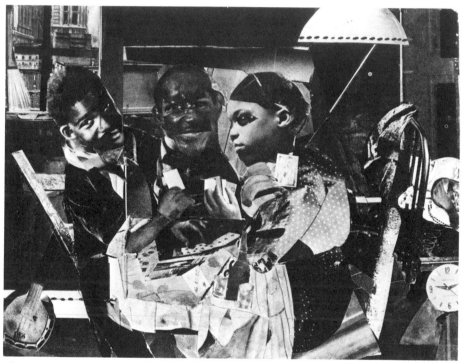

Romare Bearden (1914 -). *Evening, 9:10, 461 Lenox Avenue,* Photo-montage. Collection. The Museum of Modern Art, New York.

Instructions:

1. Make a collection of faces, or parts of faces, from such sources as magazines, photographs, and newspapers. These faces should express a particular mood such as jealousy, hate, doubt, frustration, and happiness.

2. Arrange these faces, or parts of faces, in a pictorial composition* that conveys your chosen mood in the most imaginative, dramatic, and effective way. Consider the direction of glances when arranging the faces. Some faces will be more important in getting across the mood than others. They should be the focal points of your design. You should establish their dominance* very clearly. Less important faces should be subordinate*. The easiest type of

dominance is to place one large item in the center of the design and arrange other parts around it symmetrically*. In this project, however, you should not create a symmetrical design. Your dominant and subordinate images should be placed irregularly in an asymmetrical* design.

3. Rubber cement the faces to either construction paper or cardboard measuring approximately 14" x 18". Be sure you have considered colors, sizes, and shapes that go well together in an asymmetrical design.

4. Submit for evaluation your photo-montage of a group of faces that convey a particular mood.

Learning Outcomes:

1. Discuss how the faces you have chosen, and their placement in the composition, express the mood you wish to convey.
2. Explain how the balance in your photo-montage is asymmetrical.
3. Make an asymmetrical 14" x 18" photo-montage.

Suggested Materials:

Cardboard or construction paper; scissors; rubber cement; magazines, newspapers, etc.

59

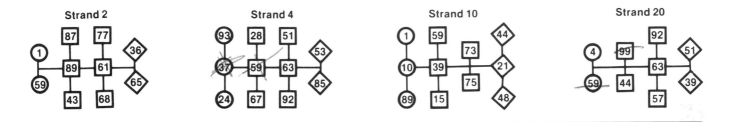

Student photo-montage of faces.

People communicate with each other most often through written words, spoken sounds, and visual images. A large cross standing in front of a building tells us that it is a church. A shield or star on the side of a car, especially when the car is painted black and white, is a symbol* for law and order. An illuminated sign* displayed prominently on a freeway tells drivers that a particular oil company has a filling station nearby. Visual symbols and signs are present wherever we look. Fast food restaurants, automobile companies, military units, political parties, states and nations all make extensive use of them. Artists often design symbols and signs and also include them in pictures.

Instructions:

1. Search the area around where you live for ten very different symbols and signs that communicate a particular meaning. Avoid images where words, initials, or mathematical symbols are the most noticeable parts. No more than half of your collection is to identify commercial organizations. At least half, therefore, are to be of shapes or objects that are intended to convey abstract ideas such as "truth," "freedom," and "faith."

2. When you have found suitable images you may photograph them, draw them, photocopy them, or cut them out. At least half are to be carefully executed drawings.

3. Assemble all ten images to make a pleasing design on a sheet of paper and paste them down with rubber cement. Write or type explanations next to each of the images in your collection that describes the location where it was found and also the message that the image communicates.

   The placement and neatness of these explanations should be as much a part of the design of the presentation as the arrangement of the pictures.

4. Submit for evaluation the collection of ten signs and symbols mounted on a sheet of paper.

Cattle brands. Courtesy Dover Publications.

128

Learning Outcomes:

1. Identify ten non-verbal signs and symbols in the area in which you live.
2. Arrange five drawings and five photocopies of signs and symbols, with captions that explain their meaning and location, in a pleasing design.

Suggested Materials:
White paper; pencil and eraser; pen or typewriter; rubber cement

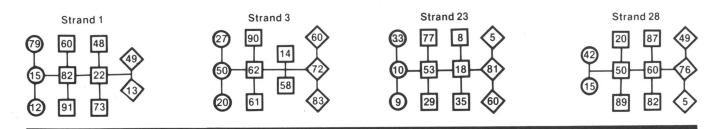

Japanese crests. Courtesy Dover Publications.

61

mixed breeding

Futuristic biologists today speak in terms of test-tube babies, cloning, and choosing genetic traits at will. And yet, for years some artists have shown through their art what biologists are just beginning to think about. One way artists have shown the combination of various ideas is through combining different body parts to portray both fantastic animals and diabolical and sublime figures. Historical examples of this kind of creativity in Greek and Roman art include the flying horse Pegasus, man-horse centaurs, the grotesque woman Medusa with snakes for hair, as well as many others from places such as Egypt, Africa, and Pre-Columbian America. In contemporary art work, surrealist* artists continue to convey fantastic ideas and dreamlike states of mind through new and exciting imagery.

This lesson provides you with the opportunity to work in this artistic tradition and to create your own fantastic images, by selecting human, animal, or plant parts and combining them to create startling, dramatic new life forms.

Student creation of a new life form.

Instructions:

1. Make at least two pencil studies depicting various plants, animals, or humans. Make the drawings as realistic as possible. For the best results, draw carefully from real objects. If this is not possible, use clear, detailed photographs. Be sure to show a full range of shading*, from very light to very dark to reveal the solidness and roundness of parts of your creature. Also, include as many details as possible.

2. Combine parts from at least two different pencil drawings to create a new living form. Your new life form could result in a humorous, grotesque, or mysterious image. As you work on your invention, give as much attention to surface details as you give to the overall solidness of the object. Remember that the whole invention should look as though all the parts belong together; that is, the work possesses unity.*

3. Submit for evaluation at least two pencil studies of plants, animals, or humans, and any photographs or photocopies you used, together with the final drawing of your new life form.

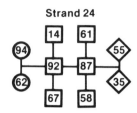

Learning Outcomes:

1. List at least three mythical mixtures of animals and plants from the history of art.
2. Explain why you chose your combination of parts to create your new life form.
3. Draw at least two plants, humans, or animals. Create a single new living form using a full range of shading and detailed surface features.

Suggested Materials:

White drawing paper; 2B, 4B, 6B pencils and eraser

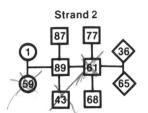

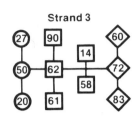

Student creations of new life forms.

the art of greece and rome

Much of our present day civilization originated in ancient Greece and Rome. The arts and sciences that characterize the western world had their origins during this period, which reached its height over two thousand years ago. The ideas of Greek philosophers continue to be important in the Western world.

The art of ancient Greece and Rome frequently influences us today in the design of our buildings, in our lettering styles, and in decorations we use. You could spend many years studying the Classical* period of Greek and Roman civilizations and their influences on contemporary Western art. In this lesson, however, you will study the artistic influences of Greek and Roman styles* that are still visible in the community where you live.

Instructions:

1. Study pictures of all kinds of Greek and Roman art in books from your library. Take a walk around your community in search of examples of art that show the influence of Classical Greek and Roman designs.

2. Make careful drawings of at least two very different objects that show Classical influences in your community. Draw the objects along with other objects that surround them. Make the objects look as realistic as possible. Include shading, details, and proportions* of your objects as they appear in their surroundings. Fill 2 entire 8'' x 10'' sheets of paper with your drawings.

3. Be prepared to describe where you found the objects and to explain your reasons for believing that the design of these objects is derived from Greek and Roman art. Also, describe how well these objects fit into their present surroundings.

4. Submit for evaluation at least two accurate pencil drawings of objects from your local community that show ancient Greek and Roman influences.

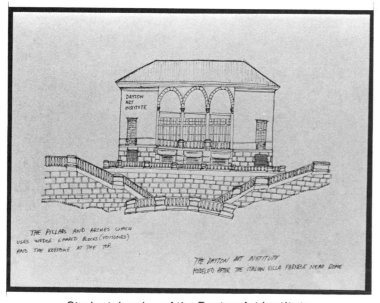

Student drawing of the Dayton Art Institute.

Student drawing of a capital on a local building.

Learning Outcomes:

1. Explain why examples of objects found in your community have their origins in classical art.
2. Describe how successfully the objects you drew fit into their present surroundings.
3. Make two accurate 8" x 10" drawings of art from your local community that reveal qualities derived from Classical art.

Suggested Materials:

White paper; pencil and eraser; pen and ink

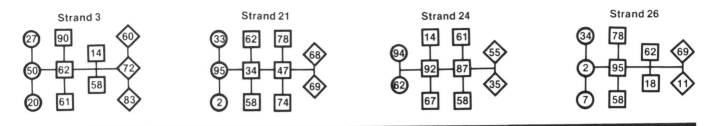

Strand 3   Strand 21   Strand 24   Strand 26

Madewood Plantation. (1840-1848). Napoleonville, LA. Courtesy Louisiana Tourist Development Commission.

63

caricature

Today it is almost impossible to look through a newspaper and not come across a caricature* of either the president or some other well-known person. Political caricatures are especially popular around election times. A caricature of an individual is based on distortion* and exaggeration* of one or more of a person's peculiarities. The purpose is generally to ridicule or to engage in satire and consequently it could be most unkind to make a caricature of a sensitive person.

The art of caricature has grown in relation to the growth of personal liberty and the advancement of mass communications. This lesson will give you an opportunity to make a caricature in which drawing is used as a weapon that is often more incisive than words could ever be.

Instructions:

1. Make a collection of at least six caricatures of well-known persons. Look in newspapers and magazines. Select those drawn in distinctly different styles*. Cut them out neatly and paste them on a sheet of paper with rubber cement so that you can study them simultaneously. Study the body similarities and differences among characteristics of the people selected. Identify differences in distortion and exaggeration upon which the artists chose to concentrate and take note of the various drawing styles they employed.

2. Now select a person for study. It could be yourself, a famous person, or someone you see every day. It should *not* be one of the people that appeared in your collection of caricatures.

   Study this person's characteristics and decide which ones make him or her a unique looking individual. Complete at least six trial caricatures, each of which exaggerates some different physical uniqueness of that person. Refer to your collection of six professional caricatures for help with drawing techniques. You may use pencil, pen and ink, or felt tipped pens to make your drawings.

3. Make two final caricature drawings based on your trial drawings that use distortion and exaggeration effectively. Fill two 6" x 8" sheets of paper with your final drawings. Be prepared to explain how the finished caricatures capture the character of your model.

4. Submit for evaluation the sheet of six professional caricatures, the six trial drawings, and your two final caricature drawings.

Finished student caricatures.

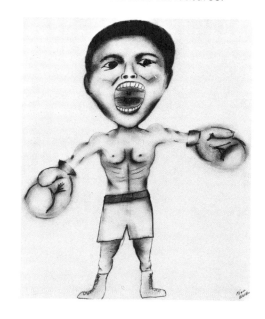

Learning Outcomes:

1. Define *caricature* as it is applied to visual art.
2. Describe differences in style of six caricatures by different artists.
3. Explain which of the two final caricatures is more successful than the other.
4. Draw at least six trial caricatures and two 6'' x 8'' final ones of a person you have selected to study.

63

Suggested Materials:

White drawing paper; pencil and eraser; pen and ink; rubber cement

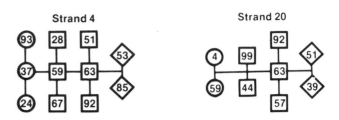

Ben Shahn. *Dr. J. Robert Oppenheimer* (1954). Brush and ink. Collection, The Museum of Modern Art, New York.

Gary Hoff, Head (Joe Ruffo): Courtesy of the artist.

coil pot construction

Clay can be molded by hand to create an infinite number of forms; but immediately people want to construct something that is larger than their hands. They have to devise special building techniques. The most ancient technique of this kind—one that continues to be used throughout the world—is coil construction. Coil pots can be small, but they can also be so large that a child can work on the inside while the father works on the outside.

This lesson instructs you on how to make a simple coil pot. With practice your skill will develop. Also with practice, you will begin to develop creative ideas of your own about coil pot construction.

Instructions:

1. To make a base for your coil pot, flatten a small piece of clay and cut it into a circle about ³/₈" thick and 3" to 4" in diameter. Remove excess clay after you cut the circle.

2. Make clay coils* by rolling a small ball of clay on a slightly damp wooden board. Roll the clay from the center of the ball outward until the coils are about ½" thick. The board should be kept damp so the clay will not dry out.

3. Circle the upper edge of the clay base with a coil of clay and join the ends together neatly. As you position this coil and all the ones that follow—roughen the clay surfaces* that are to be joined together. As you attach the coil, smear a creamy mixture of clay and water (called slip*) over these surfaces to ensure a permanent bond.

4. Continue the building process by placing a second coil on top of the first one. If you decide to make the pot curve outwards, place the coils on the outside edges of the previous coils. If you decide to make the pot curve inwards, place the coils on the inside edges of the previous coils.

   Build two pleasing but differently shaped coil pots, each of which is about 10" high. When you have completed building your pots, either smooth the outside surfaces or let all or some of the coils show. Make this decision based on the shape of the pots and what kind of decoration will best suit their forms.

5. When the finished pots are completely dry they will be hard but very brittle. To make them permanent they will need firing in a kiln to be transformed into pottery. The final stage is to glaze the surfaces to make them water tight as well as more decorative. Firing and glazing are optional for completing this lesson.

6. Submit for evaluation two different but pleasingly shaped 10" coil pots that are dry with all parts securely joined together.

The beginning stages of a coil pot.

Finished student coil pot.

Learning Outcomes:

1. Explain the technique for making a coil pot.
2. Give reasons why the two pots have pleasing shapes.
3. Make two different 10" coil pots.

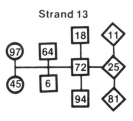

Suggested Materials:

Water based clay; water in a bowl, newspaper, paper towels; a container of slip; wooden board; optional: access to a kiln, glaze, brush

Strand 13

Paula Ahmad: Courtesy of the artist.   Coil pot with surface decoration.

65   coloring the world with feeling

When the color fades from your television set your reaction to the television program becomes different. Many of our reactions to spectacular science fiction space programs is due to the use of setting and color. In the early 20th century, Expressionist* painters used color as a powerful emotional force. They did away with natural appearances by intensifying colors and exaggerating and twisting forms to express inner truths. Expressionist painters such as Franz Marc, Paul Klee, and Paula Modesohn-Becker expressed objects in color and form as symbolic of intense emotion. In this lesson, you will learn that reality can become unreal when it is colored imaginatively.

Instructions:

1. Go outdoors and find a scene that interests you. On a sheet of heavy drawing paper, lightly draw the scene. Consider foreground*, middleground*, and background*. (See diagram on page 223.) Include as many details as possible. Cover the entire paper with objects in the scene. Arrange the composition* so that it appears balanced and holds your interest.

2. Paint the scene with tempera paints, magic markers, crayons, or watercolors. Use color to change the real colors of the scene to a scene in which color expresses the mood and emotionality of things seen. Think about how intensified colors, such as orange sky or purple shadows on a lake, make the real world have an inner life.

3. Submit for evaluation a painting of a scene in which color is used to express the mood and feeling a scene imparts.

Student painting that expresses mood in an outdoor scene.

65

Learning Outcomes:

1. Explain how Expressionist painters used color to make the real world become unreal.
2. Describe how you used intensified color to create a specific mood in your painting of a scene.
3. Paint a scene, drawn from a real scene, in which color is used to create an emotionally charged environment.

Suggested Materials:

Heavy drawing paper; pencil and eraser; tempera paint, magic markers, crayons, or watercolors

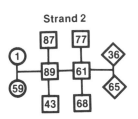

Strand 2

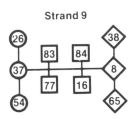

Strand 9

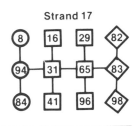

Strand 17

Franz Marc (1880-1916). *Yellow Cow.* Oil on canvas. Photo: Robert E. Mates. Collection The Solomon R. Guggenheim Museum, New York.

66

a portrait of your shoe

Throughout history drawing has played an important role in the work of architects, painters, and sculptors. Drawings were first used as preparatory sketches for a finished painting, piece of sculpture, or building. During the Renaissance, people began to collect artists' drawings because they showed an artists' personal style and also a directness of artistic expression. From the beginning of the 16th century, artists made drawings of a variety of different objects and people that were viewed as finished products and not as sketches for other art works. Today, artists continue to use many different objects as the subjects of their finished drawings. They draw objects such as tea pots, coke bottles, and car seats, as well as portraits of wealthy people. The most significant everyday objects can be made important through an artist's drawing. Your task in this lesson is to make a finished drawing after careful observation.

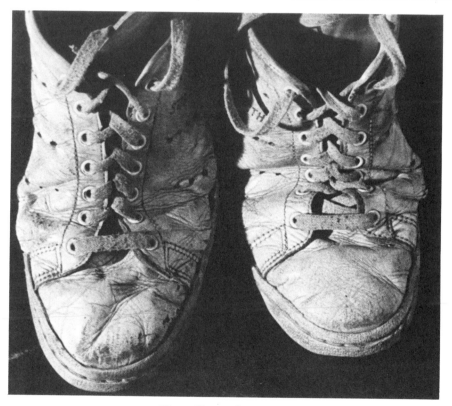

Photo: Harvey Osterhoudt.

Instructions:

1. On a piece of white drawing paper, using a #2 or 4B pencil, practice making a variety of different kinds of lines such as vertical, horizontal, wavy, curved, bent, short, long, broken, continuous, thick, and thin lines. See how many different kinds of lines you can create. Fill a sheet of paper with these experiments.

2. Remove one of your shoes. Place it on the table in front of you. Look at its overall shape. Observe details such as a worn heel, frayed shoelace, missing eyelet, and bent tongue that make it your shoe.

3. On a minimum 10" x 12" sheet of white drawing paper, draw an outline of the shape of your shoe. Once the shape is correct, draw all the details you can see. Use a selection of the varied line experiments you created to draw these details. Concentrate on the line quality of your drawing, then add shading*. Draw the shoe so that it fills the drawing paper. Try to capture your shoe's personality.

4. Submit for evaluation the sheet of line experiments and your finished pencil drawing of your shoe.

Learning Outcomes:

1. Explain why drawings of everyday objects can be considered finished art works.
2. List details in your drawing that show your shoe possesses a personality of its own.
3. Create a 10" x 12" detailed, shaded drawing of your shoe.

Suggested Materials:

White drawing paper; pencil, #2 or 4 B, and eraser

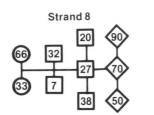

Strand 8

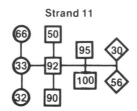

Strand 11

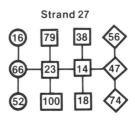

Strand 27

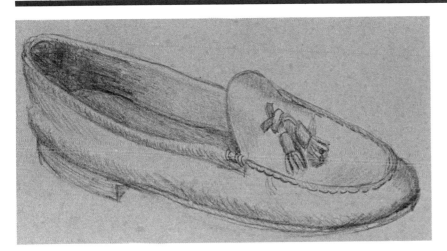

Student drawing of a shoe.

Vincent Van Gogh (1853-1890). *Three Pairs of Shoes.* Oil on canvas. Fogg Art Museum, Collection. Harvard University. Collection of Maurice Wertheim.

67

michelangelo and the italian renaissance

Although the ruins of Greek and Roman civilization existed in Europe for a thousand years, it was not until the 14th century that people showed any real interest in them. During the period of the 14th through the 16th centuries, an immense revival of interest and activity in the arts and the sciences took place.

Italy was an intellectual and artistic center during the Renaissance. Michelangelo (1475-1564)

lived at the height of this great cultural rebirth. His drawings, sculptures, and paintings exemplify Renaissance ideals. These ideals included the search for perfection, the revival of Classical* values, the scientific study of the world, and deep religious feelings. This lesson is designed to help you become familiar with drawings of people created by Michelangelo and how they reflect Renaissance ideals.

Student drawing based on a drawing by Michelangelo.

Instructions:

1. Michelangelo's drawings of people are reproduced in just about every art history book. Find a good, clear reproduction of one of them. You may choose either a portrait or a full length figure. It should be a fairly large reproduction so you can see the details clearly.

   You can understand many things about an artist's work by writing papers about his art; but if you hope to capture the true spirit of his or her work there is no substitute for trying to work in the same way the artist did.

2. Draw the Michelangelo art work you chose so that you become as familiar as possible with the way he worked. Make your drawing as identical to the original as possible. Be sure the proportions* you draw correspond with those used by Michelangelo; demonstrate how he drew lines, shading*, and details. See page 223 for a checklist of body and facial proportions. Your drawing should be large enough to fill a sheet of paper 9" x 12" or larger. Label your drawing with the title of the work by Michelangelo.

3. Submit for evaluation your rendering of a drawing by Michelangelo together with the actual reproduction you used — or a clear photocopy.

Learning Outcomes:

1. Explain why the revival of Greek and Roman art during the 14th - 16th centuries was called the Renaissance.
2. Describe qualities in Michelangelo's work that represent the ideals of Italian Renaissance art.
3. Make an accurate 9" x 12" pencil or ink study of a drawing of a person by Michelangelo.

Suggested Materials:

White paper (at least 9" x 12"); pencil and eraser; pen and ink

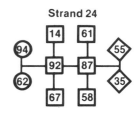

Strand 4

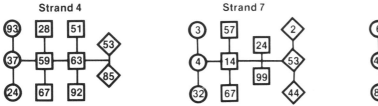

Strand 7

Strand 16

Strand 24

Student drawing based on a sculpture by Michelangelo.

Student drawing based on a painting by Michelangelo.

68 impossibles

Our eyes often play tricks particularly on those occasions when we look through special lenses or see reflected images in a warped mirror. Mirages occur in the desert as a consequence of distortions* due to heat and reflection. Refraction in water causes objects to appear to bend. The list of natural phenomena that produce optical illusions* is quite extensive. In contrast, a number of shapes which initially appear normal could never exist except as images on a sheet of paper.

Some artists have become fascinated by illusions and by optical impossibilities. Perhaps the most notable artist in this century to use optical illusions is the Dutch artist, M.C. Escher. In this lesson, you are asked to use optical illusions in your own art work.

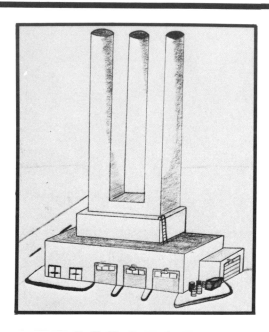

Student drawings using optical illusions.

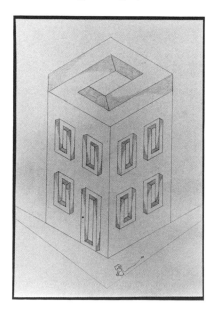

Instructions:

1. Make at least three practice drawings in which you show objects consisting of impossible shapes or optical illusions. The "impossibility" or illusory character of the shapes should be stressed. The drawings shown as examples for this lesson may be of assistance, but do not copy them.

   Using ideas in your three practice drawings, create a final drawing in which an arrangement of impossible shapes is used to create a unified* design. This picture is to be of your own invention.

2. The choice of medium* in this task is important if you are to achieve the best results. That decision will be left to you. You may find paint to be most useful. Alternatively, you may prefer a drawing medium such as pencil, pen and ink, or felt tipped pens, or any mixture of the three. Be prepared to explain your choice when asked.

3. Submit for evaluation your three practice drawings and your final art work of a picture that consists of impossible shapes or optical illusions.

Learning Outcomes:

1. Describe how M.C. Escher uses illusions and optically impossible shapes in his art work.
2. Explain how you have used specific parts of your practice drawings to create the finished art work.
3. Create an art work based on selected optical illusions or impossible shapes in which the parts go together to create a unified design; the choice of medium is your decision.

68

Suggested Materials:

Paper; any suitable pictorial medium

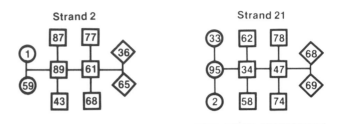

M.C. Escher. *Relativity* (1953). The National Gallery of Art, Washington. Rosenwald Collection.

architectural design

People often have mental images of a dream house. Sometimes they collect ideas from magazines that show beautifully designed homes. A no less imaginative, but probably more practical task is to visualize modifications that might be made to an existing house so that it might become more functional and attractive. These kinds of ideas need to be drawn on paper in order to share them with other people. That is the task for this lesson.

Instructions:

1. Search your community for an older home, or use a photograph of an older house that could be modernized or remodeled. The question you will ask yourself is what changes to the external appearance are likely to be necessary or desirable.

2. Using a pencil, draw the original house you have selected as accurately as you can. For the purposes of this drawing, place yourself so that one corner of the building is closest to you. You should then be able to see two sides of it clearly. The experience with two-point perspective* drawing in Lesson 78 will prove useful as you draw. Be sure that the eye level is clearly indicated. Check that the proportions*

of the house are accurate, and all details are included. Do *not* shade your drawing*.

3. Transfer the drawing to another piece of paper with tracing paper. First, trace all lines of the original drawing on the tracing paper. Turn the tracing paper over; with a blunt pencil point, cover all lines. Place the tracing paper on a sheet of paper and draw over the lines.

4. Modify the design of the traced house to serve its updated or altered function. Complete this drawing to the point that the quality of the drawing is comparable with the original drawing of the house.

5. Submit for evaluation the drawings of the original house and the altered house.

Photo: Phil Whitlow, *The Herald-Telephone,* Bloomington, Indiana.   A remodeled house.

Learning Outcomes:

1. List and explain changes you made to the original building when you remodeled it.
2. Explain how to use tracing paper correctly when transferring a drawing from one sheet of paper to another.
3. Draw a house, using two-point perspective, showing proper proportion, and including all the details of the original. Also, draw a modification of this house to show a change of function.

Suggested Materials:

White paper; tracing paper; pencil and eraser

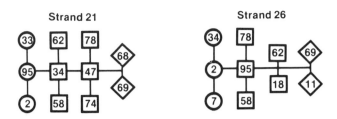

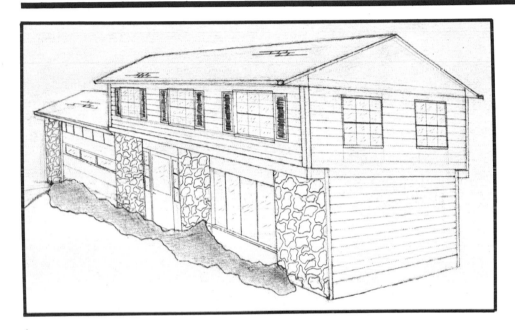

Student drawings of a house in its original and altered states.

JERRY LANDE READ PP 60

The Mexican Revolution ended 60 years ago; during the following quarter century a group of Mexican painters became internationally prominent as mural* artists. Murals are art applied to inside and outside walls of buildings. Some of these murals were painted while others were mosaics.* The scenes shown in most Mexican murals had to do with activities that went on inside the building or ideas taken from Mexican history. Themes included scenes from the time Mexico won its independence as well as great ideals such as justice, freedom, and the abolition of slavery.

A mural is designed to fit a specific wall space. As a result, it is usually a different shape than the ordinary rectangle. This lesson presents you with the task of designing a mural for some specific wall.

Instructions:

1. Find a wall which you feel would be improved if a mural were painted on it. It may be located indoors or out. Draw the shape of the wall on a large piece of paper making sure that the proportions* are correct and that details such as windows, doors, moldings, and bookshelves are included. You may use a straight edge to draw lines of the walls and other details.

2. Design a mural for that wall. The subject you choose should fit the activities that take place in the room or the building where the wall is located. A mural for a gymnasium wall, for example, should look very different from one done in a science laboratory or in a home economics room.

    Decide on a theme for your mural. Sketch all the details for your mural on your drawing of the wall. Plan a well organized composition. Decide what colors you will use. Your colors can be dull or bright. The mural can be peaceful or full of action. Think of all the things that could affect how you want the mural to look. Remember that repetition of shapes, lines, and colors can help to unify* your mural.

3. Complete your mural design with paint, crayon, or felt markers so that it could be enlarged and painted on a wall. It should be executed carefully and demonstrate your imaginativeness in expressing a theme to be used on a wall in a specific location.

4. Submit for evaluation a mural design in color that could be enlarged to fit a specific wall.

José Clemente Orozco (1883 - 1949). *Anglo-America and Hispano-America.* Fresco. Panels 10 and 11 of the murals in the Baker Library, Dartmouth College.

Learning Outcomes:

1. Define the word mural.
2. List some themes Mexican mural artists used during the second quarter of the 20th century.
3. Explain the meaning of your mural and its suitability to a particular wall.
4. Design a color mural concerned with a specific theme to fit a particular wall.

70

Suggested Materials:

White paper, at least 18" x 24"; pencil and eraser; felt markers; crayons; paints and brushes; mixing tray; water; paper towels; ruler

Strand 8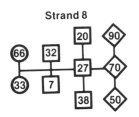

Strand 12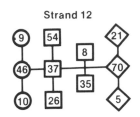

Strand 22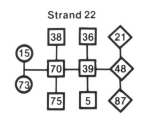

Diego Rivera (1886-1957). *The Grand Tenochtitlan* (now Mexico City). Fresco. The National Palace, Mexico City.

A view of the Rivera mural across the courtyard.

71   appliqué wall hanging

A wall hanging is usually a decorated textile that is designed to be suspended on a wall to enhance its appearance. People often prefer wall hangings to more conventional art work such as paintings and drawings. One popular way of making a wall hanging is to use appliqué techniques*. Appliqué involves cloth pieces of various kinds that are stitched on a cloth background. You will be able to try your hand at creating an appliqué wall hanging in this lesson.

Instructions:

1. Arrange pieces of colored paper to make a design plan. The images may be derived from natural objects such as flowers, trees, leaves or waves. They may also be shapes from manmade objects such as houses, cars, or people. Appliqué designs usually look best if simplified shapes are used. When creating your plan for an appliqué design, pay attention to the silhouettes* of the shapes you have chosen. Repeat shapes, colors, and textures to achieve unity* in the design.

2. Collect pieces of cloth of varied color, shape and texture that complement the image in your plan. Cut them into shapes based on your plan and place them on a fabric background. Since the cloth pieces are silhouettes, your design will divide the background* cloth into new spaces. Arrange the pieces of cloth so that the areas of background that remain create an interesting design. Remember to use repeated shapes, colors, and textures to achieve unity in your appliqué design.

3. As a test of your sensitivity toward the background space make a sketch showing only the background spaces. If some background spaces appear awkward you may move your pieces of cloth to improve these spaces.

4. The pieces of cloth should now be neatly stitched to the background. The stitches that decorate the edges of the cloth should be planned as integral parts of the appliqué design. Stitches can also be used to add decorations to other parts of the cloth pieces and background.

5. When the design is finished, roll or loop the top edge and stitch the bottom edge. Run a dowel or other straight stick through the loop that is created. The hanging is then ready to be displayed on a wall.

6. Submit for evaluation your cut paper design, the sketch of the background, and the finished appliqué wall hanging.

Student appliqué work.

Learning Outcomes:

1. Define appliqué with reference to wall hangings.
2. Describe how the paper design and sketch of the background are related to your finished appliqué wall hanging.
3. Design and execute an appliqué wall hanging based on a cut paper plan of shapes derived from natural or man-made objects.

Suggested Materials:

Scissors; needle; collection of varied pieces of fabric; a large piece of fabric (background); yarn, silk, thread, etc.; dowel (or even a fairly straight branch)

Strand 5

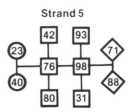

Strand 14

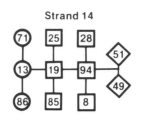

Strand 18

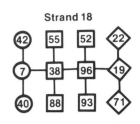

Student appliqué work.

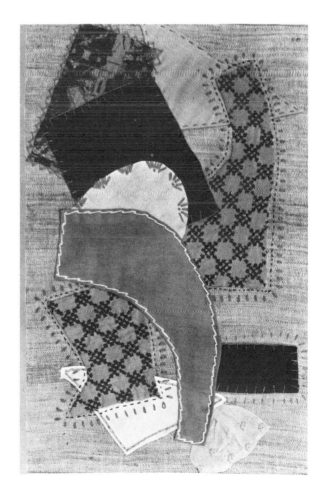

151

carving

For centuries, small children, old people, skilled craftspersons, and artists in all parts of the world have whittled or chipped away at scraps of hard wood with sharp knives. The result of such efforts can lead to the production of a pleasing piece of sculpture. Craftspersons in parts of Kentucky and Tennessee today make and sell beautiful carvings of animals, people, and plants, and earn part or all of their livings in this way. However, sharp knives can also cut the carver, so considerable care and skill is needed when carving a sculpture.

In this lesson you are to carve a plant or an animal from a material of your choice.

Instructions:

1. Softer materials than wood can be carved that do not require the sharp tools that are used for carving hardwood. These include wax blocks, soap, clay, plaster, and various soft woods. Select the kind of material you prefer. The piece of material should be large enough to create a finished carving.

2. Make a top view, front view, and side view sketch on paper to decide how the plant or animal is to look. Pictures of historical examples from Africa and Egypt may provide some ideas you may want to use.

3. Draw or scratch the approximate shape directly onto the block to be carved. First draw the side view, then the top view, and last the front view. Make the shape fill the block as completely as possible.

4. The work of carving is slow and painstaking. It requires that the block be carefully reduced to the desired shape with a sharp tool such as a knife. Pieces cut off by mistake cannot be attached again successfully. The final product may be waxed, polished, or stained depending on the material you choose.

5. Submit for evaluation the top, side, and front view sketches and the finished carving of a plant or animal.

John B. Flannagan (1898-1942) *Chimpanzee.* Granite. Collection of Whitney Museum of American Art, New York.

Learning Outcomes:

1. List places where craftspersons have established a tradition of woodcarving.
2. Explain how your sketch ideas for a carving were transformed into a carving.
3. Make a finished carving of a plant or animal in a material of your choice.

Suggested Materials:

Sharp knife, rasp*, sandpaper; block of material to carve: wood, (preferably soft), paraffin wax block, piece of soap, hard or nearly hard clay, plaster, or commercial products that resemble stone, wood, or metal; paper; pencil and eraser; wax, stain, etc.

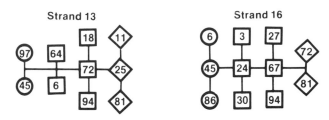

Strand 3

Strand 13

Strand 16

A plaster block marked for three stages of carving.

Alaskan Eskimo (19th century). *Walrus.* Indiana University Museum. Photo: David Schalliol.

73

opposites

Have you ever thought about the numbers of ideas and beliefs you possess? Sometimes, defining one of your ideas can require that you also understand its opposite. For example, being able to explain "evil" is likely to mean that you also have an understanding of the meaning of "good." Some other examples of these opposite ideas are civilized and barbaric, heaven and hell, innocent and worldly, optimism and pessimism, male and female.

A good test of a person's understanding occurs when he or she tries to communicate with someone else. Since this is an art course, the task here is for you to express visually an idea or belief and its opposite.

Instructions:

1. Art is expressed through various media* by means of the elements of lines, colors, textures, shapes, and space*. They are all used together in different ways to convey ideas and emotions. They result in creative compositions. If you think for a moment about one of your sets of opposite ideas, it is likely to suggest certain qualities of different art elements. Opposite word meanings are likely to suggest art elements that possess characteristics that are opposite such as bright and dull, rough and smooth, etc.

2. The task you face is to make two visual art works where each embodies an idea that contrasts with the other. The selection of opposites is to be entirely your own as is your choice of images.

Your art may be representational*, or abstract*, or non-objective*. You may be able to capture the true feelings you want to express more easily if you do not make the objects in your art work look realistic. Alternatively, you may wish to make your art work realistic. Or you may distort parts of your composition. Distortion* is a useful device for emphasizing differences. Special attention should be paid to the art elements of line, color, texture, shape, and space needed to communicate your ideas. You may express yourself in any medium* or a combination of media* that in your judgment best communicates your ideas.

3. Submit for evaluation two art works done in your choice of medium, each of which expresses an idea that is opposite from the other.

Two student works representing love and hate.

154

Learning Outcomes:

1. List the art elements you used to create your composition.
2. Explain how the elements in each of your art works express opposite ideas or beliefs.
3. Explain how the choice of media are well suited to the message expressed in each art work.
4. Make two art works that express opposite ideas.

Suggested Materials:
Your choice.

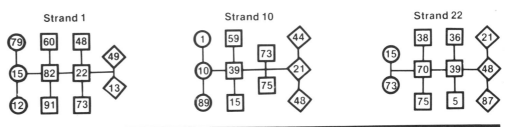

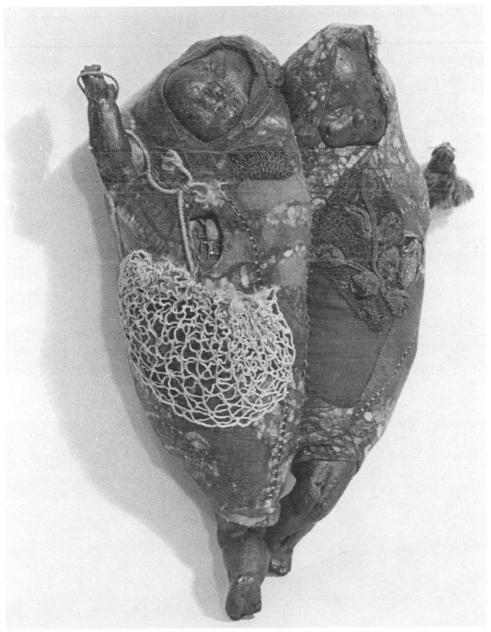

Enid Zimmerman. *Janus figure: The Past and the Future.* Courtesy of the artist. Photo: Kyu-Sun Rhee.

74

household objects

People's homes are full of manufactured objects such as televisions, telephones, tables, chairs, lamps, kitchen stoves, refrigerators, and beds. The constant presence of these objects notwithstanding, most people have little or no idea about what they really look like. Visually well educated people, on the other hand, can either describe them or draw them. Designers and architects, in particular, become very well informed about how household objects look. Painters and illustrators, whose work includes the interiors of homes, also become proficient at drawing these objects.

In this lesson, you are to study a common household object to the point where you can draw it accurately. In this way, you will have practiced drawing a household object which you might choose to include in future art work.

Instructions:

1. Select a household object that interests you and draw it. If you are not skillful at drawing, choose a side view. If you have more confidence, choose a view that shows more of the object than can be seen from the side.

    Regardless of the view, draw every part of the object that is visible. Be sure that the proportions* are accurate, that all the solid parts are drawn, that all details are shown, and that shading* is included.

2. When one view of the object is completed, make two more drawings from different views. You might choose angles from the front, back, sides, or even views looking down at the object.

3. Submit for evaluation the three different views of the household object you have chosen to draw.

Learning Outcomes:

1. Explain what you learned about drawing a household object from three different points of view.

2. Draw three different views of a household object with special attention to the accuracy of proportions, details, and shading.

Suggested Materials:

Paper; pencil and eraser

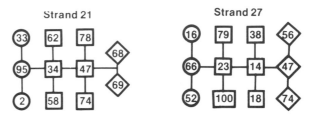

Strand 21

33   62   78
              68
95 — 34 — 47 —
              69
2   58   74

Strand 27

16   79   38   56
66 — 23 — 14 — 47
52   100   18   74

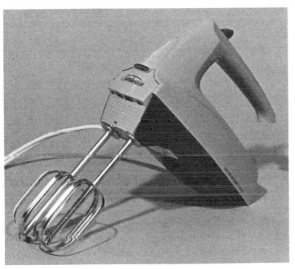

Photo: Kyu-Sun Rhee

Photo: Kyu-Sun Rhee

Photo: Kyu-Sun Rhee

gauguin

For many people all painting and sculpture that does not look realistic is called "modern art." And yet, Western artists have been creating abstract* paintings and sculpture for about the last hundred years. It is difficult to think of calling this art "modern," and yet that is what often happens.

The work of three artists was very important about a century ago. At that time paintings were beginning to look less realistic. These men were Paul Cézanne, Vincent Van Gogh, and Paul Gauguin. They had a great influence on artists who followed them and are often known as the fathers of all the abstract art that has been done since.

Their lives were all very different; you may enjoy reading about them. In this lesson, you will concentrate on the art produced by one of these great artists, Paul Gauguin.

Instructions:

1. Paul Gauguin was an intense artist whose pictures were primarily a vehicle for communicating deep emotional and spiritual feelings. His pictures are composed of large, flat areas painted in strong, luminous colors that often clash sharply with each other.

   In the latter part of the 19th century, Gauguin left France to live on the island of Tahiti in the South Pacific. The style he had developed earlier came to its full maturity in this colorful tropical environment. Together with Vincent Van Gogh, Gauguin's art became the foundation for later Expressionist* painters in the 20th century.

2. Study as many works of art by Paul Gauguin as you can. Most libraries have art books in which you will find color plates of his paintings. The black and white pictures shown with this lesson may also help you although they lack the important quality of color.

3. Paint a picture of a place or a person you know. This picture is to be entirely your own work; however, it is to be painted with the color range and in the emotional and spiritual style of Gauguin. Keep one or more reproductions by Gauguin next to you as you work.

4. Submit for evaluation at least two photocopies or reproductions of paintings by Gauguin and a painting using his color range and emotional and spiritual style.

Paul Gauguin (1848-1903). *The Yellow Christ.* Oil on canvas. Albright-Knox Art Gallery. Buffalo, New York.

Learning Outcomes:

1. Describe how Gauguin's pictures communicate emotional and spiritual feelings.
2. Explain how the color, emotional, and spiritual style of your painting resembles the style used by Gauguin.
3. Paint an original picture in Gauguin's style.

Suggested Materials:

White paper; pencil and eraser; any paint medium, palette, brushes; water, paper towels

75

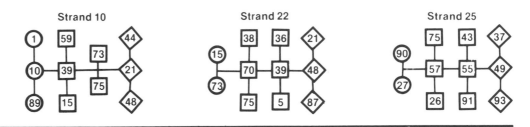

Strand 10

Strand 22

Strand 25

Paul Gauguin. *Fatata te Miti* (By the Sea). Oil on canvas. National Gallery of Art, Washington. Chester Dale Collection.

76

stencil design

Stenciling is a very practical way to print such things as notices and textile* designs. It also offers opportunities for creative problem solving. Paint is dabbed or brushed across a sheet of thin but strong (usually waxed) cardboard out of which shapes have been cut. The cut-out spaces make the design. "Bridges" across the larger cut spaces are necessary in order to hold the stencil card in one piece. The bridges can also be used to enhance a design when incorporated as part of the plan. A stencil design can be very effective when used repeatedly as in textile designs or singly when making posters or greeting cards. In this lesson you will create a stencil design to be used in a repeated pattern.

Instructions:

1. Design an original symbol for yourself that captures your personality, professional hopes, or some combination of the two. Instead of using your name or initials, develop the design from images with which you identify. A scuba enthusiast's design might be based on air tanks or flippers. A future electronics engineer might develop a design on printed circuitry.

   The design of the symbol should be small and fairly simple, because it is to be cut out and printed so as to identify personal articles such as books or suitcases.

2. First, cut a small sample piece of stencil cardboard with a sharp X-acto knife* or single-edge razor blade. Cut on top of thick cardboard so as not to damage furniture. Put the cut stencil on a sheet of paper for printing. Print it by dabbing (not rubbing) with a stencil brush or sponge. Use fairly dry color. The objective is to make solid, clean-edged prints.

3. Now cut the stencil you designed. Using one color, print at least three clean copies of your stencil design on different colored background* papers. Then, using the most successful color background combination, print one sheet of an attractive orderly pattern arrangement of the stencil design by repeating the design at least 25 times (5 x 5). You may turn the stencil in different directions if you wish.

5. Submit for evaluation the cut stencil, three copies of the stencil design, and the final repeated stencil design.

Student single stencil print.

Learning Outcomes:

1. Describe how to create a stencil design.
2. Explain how your final stencil design uses theme, color, and shape in its repetitions.
3. Print three one color stencil copies on different colored backgrounds. Choose the best to print a repeated (at least 25 times), one color design.

Suggested Materials:

Stencil paper (thin waxed card); paper, cardboard, or fabric; pencil and eraser; paint or textile inks; stencil brush or small sponge; water; X-acto knife

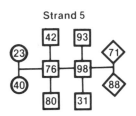

Strand 5

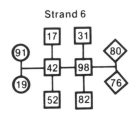

Strand 6

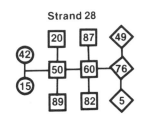

Strand 28

Student single stencil print.

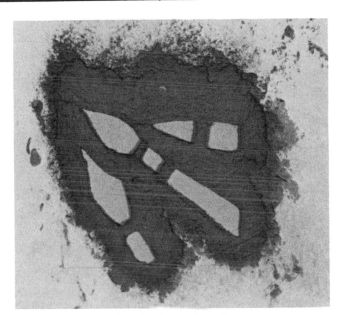

Student cut stencil.

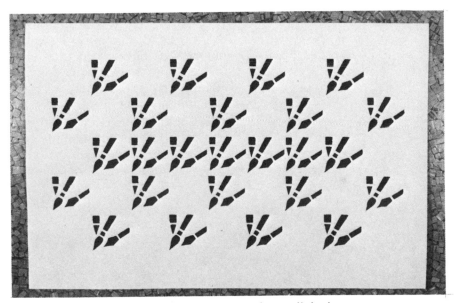

Finished student repeated stencil design.

77

the tropical jungle

Almost everyone knows what wax crayons are; most of us used them when we were children. Some professional artists continue to use wax crayons because of their brilliant colors. Wax crayons can be applied heavily; one color can be used over another. Crayoned areas can be par-tially scraped away with a sharp tool, and colors can be deliberately smudged and smeared. This lesson gives you the opportunity to explore wax crayons in many unique ways to create a jungle scene with fantastic color.

Student crayon picture of a tropical scene.

Instructions:

1. Fill two practice sheets of 8'' x 10'' paper with pencil drawings of tropical plants and birds. Books that show pictures of plant life and birds would be useful or you may go to a zoo or greenhouse for information and inspiration. Color three of the pencil drawings in different ways with wax crayons. Apply the wax crayons lightly and heavily, overlap colors, scrape away some crayon with a sharp object and use a few drops of turpentine to soften the crayons so the colors will blend.

2. Select the most successful sketches and re-draw them on a 12'' x 18'' sheet of paper to make a picture of a tropical scene. Be sure your design shows balance*, unity*, and in-cludes many interesting objects. Include a vari-ety of plants and animals that have interesting shapes and patterns*.

3. Color your plan for a crayon painting of a trop-ical scene. Use crayon techniques you have already practiced. Repeated use of color will help to unify your composition. Color should be used imaginatively without regard for the real color of the plants and animals you used as sources for your composition. Completely fill the entire sheet of paper with color and images of plants and animals.

4. Submit for evaluation the two 8'' x 10'' prac-tice sheets of pencil drawings with three colored images and the finished 12'' x 18'' cray-on picture.

162

Learning Outcomes:

1. List a variety of ways that wax crayons may be applied to drawing paper.
2. Explain why you chose some sketches as most successful and used them as the basis of your final crayon picture.
3. Make a 12" x 18" wax crayon picture of a tropical scene.

Suggested Materials:

Drawing paper, 8" x 10", 12" x 18"; pencil, eraser; wax crayons; scissors; turpentine

77

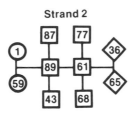

Strand 2

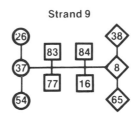

Strand 9

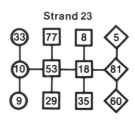

Strand 23

Henri Rousseau (1844-1910). *The Waterfall.* Oil on canvas. Courtesy of the Art Institute of Chicago, Helen Birch Bartlett Memorial Collection.

Student crayon picture of a tropical scene.

If a box-shaped object is placed so that one corner is closest to you, each of the two visible sides will no longer appear as rectangles. This effect is most noticeable when looking at buildings. The lines marking the tops and bottoms of the distorted rectangles seem to converge on each other from two directions. Vertical lines remain vertical, however. The same kind of distortion occurs indoors except that when viewing the far corner of a room the floor and ceiling lines converge toward the corner.

This lesson is designed to help you draw with what is called two-point perspective* in the easiest way possible.

Instructions:

1. Find a fairly large photograph in a magazine that shows either several simple, square-shaped buildings or an interior that shows simple, square-shaped spaces all with one corner near the center of the picture. Cut the photograph and cement it in the center of a sheet of paper that has extra space at each side.

2. Place a ruler on just the main straight horizontal edges (contours*) such as those that separate walls from ceilings and floors. Draw the edges of the shapes that extend either toward or away from you. You will see that these lines converge, that is, approach each other in two main directions.

   Extend each of these sets of lines until each comes together at what are called "vanishing points." In order to have space to show both sets of converging lines coming together it may be necessary to tape extra sheets of paper to your drawing paper.

   If it looks as though your lines will never join on your paper, select another photograph where at least some of the lines converge at vanishing points. Both of these sets of lines will cross exactly on the "eye level*" or horizon.

3. Now draw in all the other lines in the photograph to their respective vanishing points.

4. Finally, make your own drawing of the same photograph as accurately as possible. If you wish, use a ruler to help you. Be sure to show most smaller items in the original photograph.

5. Submit for evaluation a photograph with lines showing two-point perspective and your own drawing of the same photograph.

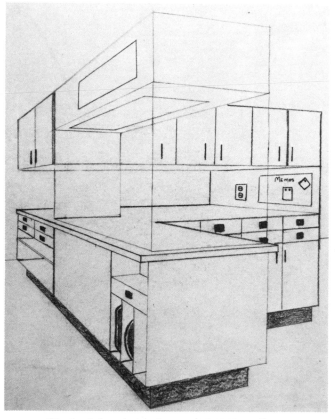

Student drawing in two point perspective.

164

Learning Outcomes:

1. Define *vanishing point.*
2. Explain when *two-point perspective* is a useful way of drawing objects.
3. Draw on top of a photograph to show how lines meet at two vanishing points; make an accurate drawing of this photograph.

78

Suggested Materials:

White paper; pencil and eraser; scissors; rubber cement; ruler; magazine illustration

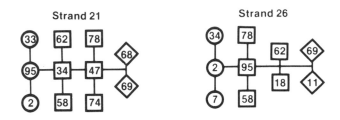

Houmas House. Greek revival mansion (1840). Burnside, LA. Courtesy Louisiana Tourist Development Commission.
The black lines show how parallel lines appear to converge with distance.

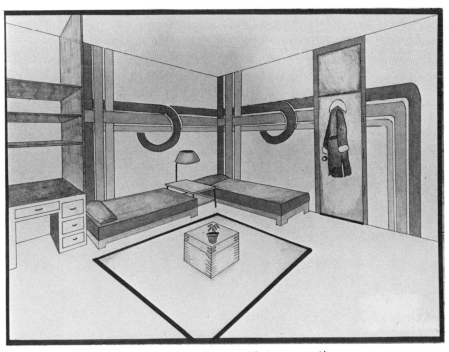

Student drawing in two point perspective.

79

The capital letters of our alphabet were developed by the Romans. The lower case or small letters appeared several hundred years later when people needed to write more rapidly. Over the centuries many variations of the basic shapes have been designed. Today, many more lettering styles* are in use than ever before, and new ones are continually being created. New styles appear because people change their ideas about what letter shapes look attractive.

When you realize that all letters have to look like the basic alphabet shapes to be readable, the presence of so many different styles shows that designers have to be highly imaginative. This lesson gives you an opportunity to be creative with the design of letter-shapes.

Instructions:

1. Study books and magazines that have advertising in them. Draw some examples of capital letters in the styles of lettering that appeal to you. Fill a carefully ruled practice sheet with accurate drawings. This experience will prepare you for designing your own alphabet style.

2. Design your own alphabet of capital (upper case) letters. Each letter must be at least ¾" tall, attractive, and easy to read. All of the 26 different shapes should look as though they belong together.

   This kind of task is a test of a person's creativity because of the strict limitations that have to be followed.

3. To see how the letters look when they are used in words, make photocopies (xerox, etc.) of the letters of your first and last name. Cut these letters out and arrange them to form your name. Take care to space the letters properly. Attach them with rubber cement to a sheet of drawing paper.

4. Submit for evaluation the full capital letter alphabet and the example of your name.

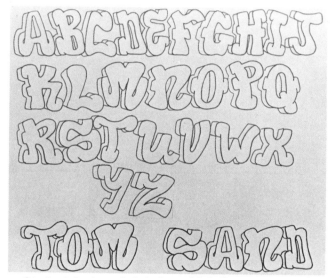

Student designed alphabet with full name xeroxed.

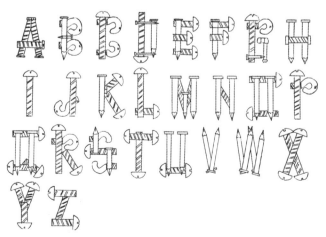

Student designed alphabet.

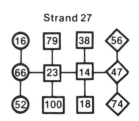

Learning Outcomes:

1. Define *upper-case* as used in lettering.
2. Explain how elements of the 26 different shapes of your letters make them appear to belong together.
3. Design an alphabet of at least ¾'' tall upper case letters. Print your name in this style.

Suggested Materials:

Drawing paper; C-2 or C-3 speedbal pen points; black ink; paints, brushes; water, paper towels; rubber cement; pen holder.

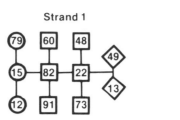
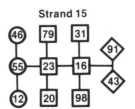

Strand 1

```
(79)  [60]  [48]
          
(15)─[82]─[22]──<49>
                <13>
(12)  [91]  [73]
```

Strand 15

```
(46)  [79]  [31]
                <91>
(55)─[23]─[16]──
                <43>
(12)  [20]  [98]
```

Strand 27

```
(16)  [79]  [38]  <56>
                  
(66)─[23]─[14]──<47>
                  
(52)  [100] [18]  <74>
```

Student designed alphabet with first name xeroxed.

167

printmaking as a fine art

Printmaking is one of the Fine Arts, together with painting, drawing, sculpture, and architecture. Prints have their own special character depending on the process being used. Screenprints* (often called serigraphs) look different from lithographs*, engravings* or wood cuts*. Linoleum block prints are identified by the marks made by the tool used to cut into the linoleum and also by the raggedness of the edges of the cut linoleum. This lesson introduces you to the art of making linoleum block prints, where the cutting process goes through several stages before being complete. The final result is a series of signed prints called an edition*.

Instructions:

1. Find a simple geometric* design from another part of the world, another culture, or from another time in history. It could be of an animal or a plant, or it could be non-objective* and not resemble anything. Make a photocopy of the design. On a sheet of drawing paper modify the design so that it fits a rectangle measuring 4" x 6". At this stage the design should be quite simple.

    Think carefully about the areas around the design, the negative* spaces, as well as the design itself, the positive* space. Both positive and negative spaces should look in balance* with each other.

2. Transfer the design onto a linoleum block of the same size. The easiest way to do this is to place carbon paper between the design and linoleum and draw over the design. Use a light colored linoleum block or cover the linoleum with white tempera to show more clearly the transferred lines.

3. Remove a small part of the design with linoleum cutters, perhaps some small shapes and a few lines. Cut fairly deeply but avoid exposing the jute backing. Keep your fingers behind the tools as you cut. Then cut the larger lines and shapes. Wash the white paint off the block in preparation for printing.

4. Spread a small amount of dark colored printing ink in a thin even layer on a sheet of glass or plastic, using a hard cloth pad or roller called a brayer. The ink is then rolled or dabbed evenly to cover the surface of the block.

5. Place a piece of thin white paper on the inked linoleum. Gently but firmly rub the paper all over with the rounded bottom of a spoon. Carefully lift a corner of the paper. If the print looks good, lift the paper gently from the block. Make three good prints before washing the block clean. Then, paint the block white again, and retrace the design on the surface.

6. Cut away more parts of the design to make it complete and balanced. Then make three more prints this time using a dark colored ink and different colors of paper.

7. Submit for evaluation the three preliminary prints, the three final prints, the design, and the linoleum block.

Printing ink being spread on a glass sheet with a brayer.

Removing linoleum with a cutter.

Learning Outcomes:

1. Explain why printmakers make many prints before they sign a finished edition.

2. Describe the process of transferring a design to a linoleum block and cutting a design in two or more stages.

3. Print an edition of three finished prints in one dark colored ink on differently colored papers.

80

Suggested Materials:

White, thin, and carbon paper; pencil and eraser; white tempera; water soluble printing ink; brush; water; paper towels; brayer or hard pad of cloth; thick linoleum; linoleum cutters; sheet of thick glass, metal, or plastic

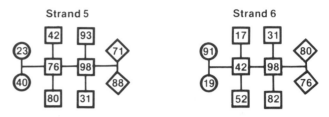

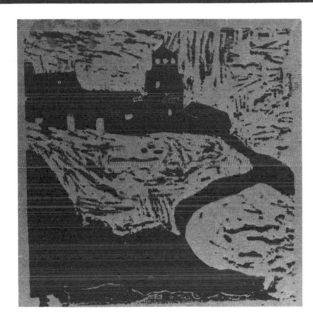 

Student linoleum block prints.

81   sculpture over an armature

A tall, thin sculpture made of clay or plaster cannot stand up by itself. It needs some kind of support. For example, people have bones inside them to support their muscles and organs. A sculptor's "skeleton" is called an armature. Sculptors often put an armature of thick wire or metal pipe inside their work for support. Chicken wire is used to help support sculpture. For small pieces you can use a wadded ball of newspaper.

This lesson is designed to introduce designing a piece of sculpture that is supported by an armature.

Frederic Remington (1861-1909). *Bronco Buster.* Bronze (from a clay model). Courtesy of The Art Institute of Chicago. Gift from Mr. Burr Robbins.

Instructions:

1. Look at people when they are engaged in an activity such as running, dancing, or throwing a ball. Then, tape or twist together pieces of heavy wire so that they resemble a person in one of those activities. This is your armature. The model should be about 10" high. Nail or staple the armature into a piece of wood so it will stand alone.

2. Cover the armature with plasticine clay until it is a suitable thickness for parts of a body. Be sure that the figure looks as though it is running, dancing, throwing something with great vigor, or in some other active pose.

   Model all the main parts of the body in their proper proportions. Study front, top, and side views. Check the angles of the legs, arms, and body.

3. Submit for evaluation a clay figurine, over an armature, in an action pose.

Student action/clay sculpture over an armature.

Learning Outcomes:

1. Define *armature*.
2. Describe how the pose of your figure suggests vigorous action.
3. Model an action pose in clay over a 10'' high armature.

81

Suggested Materials:

Plasticine clay; paper towels; newspaper; water; heavy wire; hammer, nails, etc.; block of wood; pliers

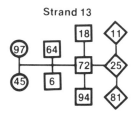

Strand 13

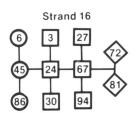

Strand 16

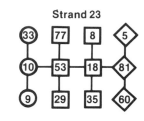

Strand 23

Mahonri M. Young. *Groggy*. Bronze (from a clay model). Collection of Whitney Museum of American Art, New York.

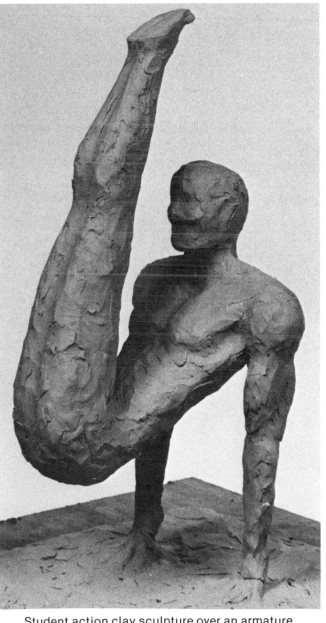

Student action clay sculpture over an armature.

171

Advertising art is all around us, on billboards, posters, television screens, magazines, and newspapers. Advertising art can be a powerful persuader influencing ideas and values such as our interpersonal relationships, products we buy, places we visit, and roles for men and women. The manner in which manufactured products are advertised both reflects and influences the public's attitudes and desires. Visual and verbal materials are unified* in such a way as to make a product attractive and desirable so we will want to buy it. In this lesson, you will choose two advertisments and analyze both their messages and artistic organization.

Instructions:

1. Look in a magazine or newspaper and choose two different advertisements that interest you. These advertisements should look different and convey different messages.
2. Answer the following sets of questions about the two advertisements:
   (a) What is the message of each advertisement? What attitudes and values are evident in the advertisement? What do they tell us about human relationships and roles in society?
   (b) How successful is each advertisement in getting the viewer's attention? How well is the lettering style matched to the illustration?
   (c) How do the two advertisements contrast and compare in terms of their messages and visual appearance? Which one is most effective and why?
3. Submit for evaluation an essay of at least three pages (1000 words) contrasting and comparing two different advertisements in the ways described above. Include xeroxes of the two advertisements.

Bruno Munari. *Campari* (1965). Offset lithograph. Collection, The Museum of Modern Art, New York. Gift of the designer.

Learning Outcomes:

1. List a number of ways that ideas and values are influenced by advertising art.
2. Explain what initially attracted you to the advertisements.
3. Write or type three or more pages (1000 words) contrasting and comparing two different advertisements.

Suggested Materials:

Writing or typing paper; pen or typewriter

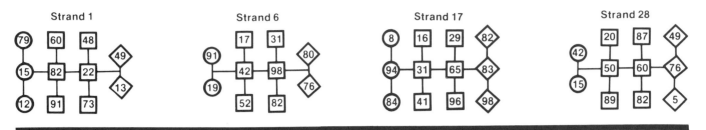

Robert Gage. *New York Is Eating It Up* (1952). Collection, The Museum of Modern Art, New York.

83

color matching collage

Some colored papers are bright and brazen. Others are much more subtle and sophisticated in their impact and include deep vibrant shades and soft tones. Paint can be mixed fairly easily to make subtle colors and gradual changes, but to do the same thing with colored papers is much more demanding.

This lesson requires that you study colors much more carefully than you might do otherwise by requiring that you find colors that exactly match those present in a colored reproduction.

Student collage of the painting, *London Bridge,* by André Derain.

Instructions:

1. Select a color reproduction of a famous painting which shows objects both near and in the distance. A large picture is easier to work from than a small one.

2. Make a collection of colored papers that correspond with the colors in the painting. Good sources include magazine illustrations, wrapping papers, construction paper, etc.

3. When you have what seems to be an adequate collection of colored papers, draw the main lines of the picture you have chosen. Now tear or cut small pieces of colored paper to match the colors in the reproduction. Paste them with rubber cement in place on your line drawing without any white paper showing.

5. Submit for evaluation the reproduction and the cut paper collage that matches it.

Learning Outcomes:

1. Explain why you selected a particular color reproduction of a famous painting for this lesson.
2. Describe any difficulties you had in matching colored papers to the colors in the reproduction.
3. Make a picture using small pieces of colored paper that match the colors in the reproduction.

Suggested Materials:

Cardboard or construction paper (12" x 18"); colored papers from many sources; pencil and eraser; scissors; rubber cement

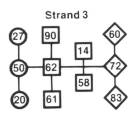

Strand 3

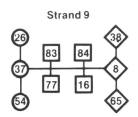

Strand 9

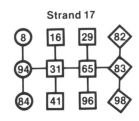

Strand 17

Student collage of the painting, *Sylvette,* by Pablo Picasso. (see below).

Pablo Picasso (1881 - 1973). *Sylvette (Portrait of Mlle. D.).* Oil on canvas. Courtesy of The Art Institute of Chicago. Gift of Mr. and Mrs. Leigh B. Block.

Student collage of the painting. *The Zouave Officer, Milliet,* by Vincent Van Gogh.

84

impressionists

In France around 1870, a group of artists became interested in how natural lighting effects occur in nature. They were called Impressionists*, and they tried to achieve the same effect with paint on canvas as one would actually experience while physically viewing fields and landscapes in natural light. They used dabbing brush techniques, and bright color schemes. They also worked quickly so as not to lose the momentary character of the scene before them. The leading painters of this movement were Edward Manet, Pierre Renoir, George Seurat, Camille Pissarro, Alfred Sisley, and Claude Monet.

The purpose of this lesson is to make a painting employing the style* of the Impressionists.

Claude Monet (1840-1926). *Le Basin d'Argenteuil.* Oil on canvas. Museum of Art, Rhode Island School of Design, Providence, Rhode Island.

Instructions:

1. Study the largest color reproductions of Impressionist paintings you can find. Observe the ways in which these artists painted. Get the feel of this style by practicing these techniques yourself. You are to copy only the method by which paint was applied; do not copy actual objects.

2. Since the Impressionists painted their finest work outdoors, you are to do the same. Sketch an outdoor scene lightly on a piece of drawing paper. Next, paint the picture in one or a combination of styles used by the Impressionist painters you have studied. You should try to use similar brush techniques and color schemes.

3. Submit for evaluation your finished picture along with the reproductions or photocopies of Impressionist art that shows the style(s) you used in your work. Also give an explanation about where the chosen style(s) can be found in your painting.

Learning Outcomes:

1. Describe the techniques Impressionist painters used to capture the effects of light and distance in nature.

2. Explain how you used a specific Impressionist painting style or styles in the picture you painted.

3. Paint a picture outdoors using the brush techniques, color, and subject matter used by Impressionist painters.

84

Suggested Materials:

Paper; pencil and eraser; paints; brushes; mixing tray; water, paper towels

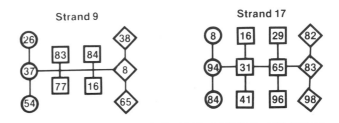

Alfred Sisley (1839-1899). *Snow at Louveciennes.* Oil on canvas. The Phillips Collection, Washington.

177

Volcanic eruptions, forest fires, great floods, hurricanes, and famines all result in terrible damage and injury. Catastrophes of this kind are often called "acts of God," because human beings cannot be held responsible for them. In contrast, a massacre is a catastrophe brought about by people. As time goes by, people become increasingly responsible for the catastrophes that occur, whether by dropping nuclear bombs or exterminating millions of people in concentration camps.

This lesson requires that you show what a catastrophe might look like at its height.

Instructions:

1. If you have ever lived through a catastrophe, you may prefer to show what you saw. Without a personal experience, you will need reference materials to suggest ideas for your picture. Books on art and the work of photo-journalists can provide useful information; your local library will have these resources. Make sketches or xerox copies of items that might be of value to you. For example, do you need an example of a tidal wave, a machine gun, a shark?

2. Organize the parts of a picture by means of several quick pencil sketches*. Imagine yourself actually a part of the catastrophe — not simply a distant observer. In this way, your personal feelings about the catastrophe are more likely to show.

3. As you develop the picture be sure that one part dominates the composition; sharpen that focal point through the use of details. Heighten the message of the picture further by means of dramatic lighting. An asymmetrical* composition* should be used since it helps create a more dramatic pictorial balance.

    Select a suitable painting medium* for the finished work. Paint it in colors designed to capture the spirit of the event.

4. Submit for evaluation the drawings and xeroxes collected as sources of visual information together with the rough sketch ideas for the finished work and the finished painting.

David Alfaro Siqueiros. *Echo of a Scream.* Duco on wood. Collection, The Museum of Modern Art, New York. Gift of Edward M.M. Warburg.

Learning Outcomes:

1. List the sources where you gathered information for a picture of a catastrophe.
2. Explain how you developed your ideas for a picture of a catastrophe.
3. Paint a dramatic picture of a catastrophe using dominance, dramatic lighting, and asymmetrical balance.

Suggested Materials:

White paper; pencil and eraser; a suitable painting medium; brushes; mixing trays; water, paper towels

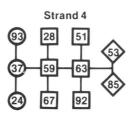

Strand 4

(93) [28] [51]
(37)—[59]—[63] ◇53◇
(24) [67] [92] ◇85◇

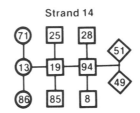

Strand 14

(71) [25] [28]
(13)—[19]—[94] ◇51◇
(86) [85] [8] ◇49◇

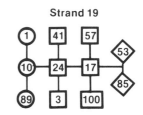

Strand 19

(1) [41] [57]
(10)—[24]—[17] ◇53◇
(89) [3] [100] ◇85◇

John Steuart Curry (1897 - 1946). *Tornado over Kansas.* Oil on canvas. Collection of Muskegon Museum of Art, Michigan.

Student pencil sketch for a finished painting.

sand casting

Cooks make jello in molds by pouring liquid into a bowl or into some specially shaped hollow container. When the jello has set, it is turned out onto a plate. The jello has been cast* into the reversed shape of the hollow mold. A hollow mold forms a solid casting.

Artists often cast objects in molds. Sculptors make plaster casts of work they have made in clay. Jewelers cast gold rings they have carved in wax. Designers make molds for casting the many kinds of plastic objects we use every day.

This lesson helps you make a cast from a simple mold you have created.

Instructions:

1. Put 2" of fine grain damp sand in a box that is about 4" deep. Make sure the surface of the sand is smooth.

2. Choose several objects that seem to go well together. Carefully press them deep into the damp sand. The resulting impressions should be grouped together to create a design where one or more parts are clearly more important than the others. Make sure the sand is wet enough to hold crisp impressions after the objects are lifted out.

3. Mix some plaster in a bowl or bucket. Put water into a bowl and sprinkle plaster into the water until it begins to show through the surface of the water. Then, mix the plaster and water together. While the plaster still flows fairly easily, gently pour it over the design you have made in the wet sand. Pour the plaster until it is at least 1" thick at the thinnest point.

   Gently press a piece of loosely woven cloth approximately the size of the box into the top surface of the plaster while it is still wet to help keep the plaster cast from breaking.

   Press a loop of string or wire fairly deeply into the plaster while it is wet so the casting can later be hung on a wall.

4. Wait at least one day for the plaster to become hard and dry before lifting the casting away from the sand. Gently brush off any sand that clings to the plaster. Store the work to permit it to dry out thoroughly.

5. Submit for evaluation a plaster relief that includes a well organized design and skill in sand casting.

Pouring plaster into an impression made by a banana in wet sand.

Learning Outcomes:

1. List objects designed by artists made by casting in molds.
2. Explain how you made your sand casting and the special skills that had to be mastered.
3. Create about a 4" thick sand casting that demonstrates a good design having one or more dominant parts.

Suggested Materials:

Newspaper; paper towels; box; sand; Plaster of Paris; water; bowl or bucket; miscellaneous objects

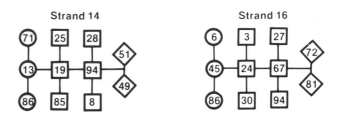

Finished student sand cast plaster reliefs.

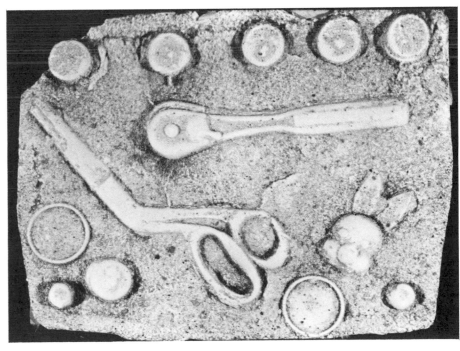

In past cultures, most people could not read; no one listened to phonographs or radios or watched television. They communicated ideas through pictures and symbols that represented ideas. In the religious art of the past in almost every culture, gods were represented symbolically by animals. The gods of ancient Babylon took such forms as the ram, bull, and crab to form the signs of the zodiac. The ancient Egyptians represented gods with cow, ram, ibis, and baboon heads. Because they symbolized gods, animals embodied the concepts of power, wisdom, faithfulness, good, and evil. In this lesson, your task will be to discuss how animals from two different cultures symbolized human characteristics.

Albrecht Dürer (1471 - 1528). *Coat of Arms with Cock.* Engraving. The Metropolitan Museum of Art, Fletcher Fund.

Instructions:

1. Look at books and find art works of animals that symbolize human characteristics such as power, wisdom, good, and evil. Choose animal symbols from two different cultures that appeal to you such as ancient Egypt, Rome, Japan, China, or Syria. Choose at least five different animals from each culture that are shown symbolically as having human characteristics.

2. Discuss, in an essay of at least three pages (1000 words), how these different characteristics became associated with each animal. Include in the essay how similar animals in the two cultures share similarities or differences associated with the characteristics they symbolize. For example, in ancient Egypt a cat symbolized serenity while in medieval Europe it symbolized evil.

3. Use rubber cement to adhere photocopies of the animals you studied to construction paper.

4. Submit for evaluation an essay about animal symbols from two cultures and mounted photocopies of at least five animal symbols from each culture.

Nootka Indian (19th century). *Thunderbird and Killer Whale.* Painting on wood. Courtesy, American Museum of Natural History. Photo: H.S. Rice.

Learning Outcomes:

1. Explain how animals in ancient cultures became symbols for various characteristics.
2. Discuss why you chose the animal symbols from the two cultures you have studied.
3. In a three page essay (1000 words), discuss, contrast, and compare your chosen symbols.

Suggested Materials:

Writing paper or typing paper; construction paper; pen or typewriter; rubber cement

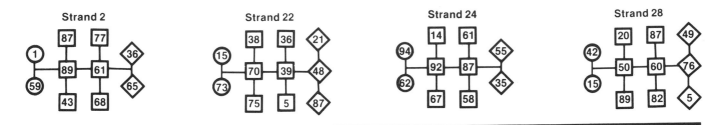

Egyptian. *The Cat Goddess, Bastet* (about 500 B.C.). Bronze with gold earrings. The Metropolitan Museum of Art.

weaving on a flat loom

The art of weaving dates back to the earliest stages of civilization. While most cloth fabric is now manufactured on power driven looms, the same principles are used today that have been used for thousands of years. While the basic process of weaving continues to remain more or less the same, designers invent ways of applying these processes to create new forms that keep pace with fashions in the clothing, drapery, and upholstery industries.

While it is not possible for you to have your designs manufactured on power looms, it is possible for you to experience small scale cloth making on a hand loom. In this way you can learn the structure of woven fabric and also experiment making your own woven designs.

Instructions:

1. Machines designed for weaving are called looms. The simplest form of loom consists of a flat rectangle of wood or cardboard. Around this rectangle in one direction is wrapped some strong yarn or string. This is called the warp.

   In this lesson you may notch two opposite edges of the board at ¼" intervals. This is usually best when using cardboard. Alternatively, you may stick headless nails or pins into wood at ¼" intervals. If you use cardboard, the pins should be inserted into the edge of the cardboard and not through it.

2. A length of colored yarn is now threaded into a blunt needle and woven over and under the warp threads from one side of the board to the other. This length of yarn (called a weft thread) is then pushed as firmly as possible up to the pins. The weft yarn is then returned to the other side of the warp in the same manner — always following the over-under action. This line of weaving is pushed firmly into the preceding line of weaving. This process continues until the weaving is finished. Weft threads should not be pulled too tight or the resulting fabric will be wide at the ends and narrow in the middle. Study the illustration to see how to construct the loom.

   As you come to the end of a length of weft thread, a new piece is tied to it, with the knot being made at the back of the textile. The final length is tied off on itself.

3. The finished weaving may be removed from the loom either by removing the nails or pins or by bending the cardboard so that the woven textile may be slipped off.

4. The first piece of weaving may be quite small. The purpose of the exercise is to ensure that you have developed enough of the basic skill to begin thinking about the design of textiles*.

A second, more elaborate piece of textile is now to be woven. It is to fill a fairly large sheet of plywood or cardboard. You are to experiment with weft yarns of several colors to create a design composed of bands of color you find pleasing.

5. Submit for evaluation a trial flat loom weaving and a larger multi-colored weaving.

Weaving on a cardboard loom.

Learning Outcomes:

1. Explain the technique of weaving on a flat loom.
2. Give reasons why the design of the more elaborate weaving is pleasing.
3. Make two pieces of well executed weaving, one of which is to be fairly large and multicolored.

Suggested Materials:

Rigid cardboard or plywood; scissors; pins, or headless nails; hammer; yarn, several colors.

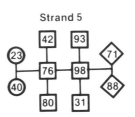

Strand 5

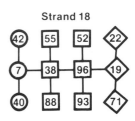

Strand 18

Student bag woven on a flat loom.

Jackie Olenick. *Weaving* (1979). Courtesy of the artist.

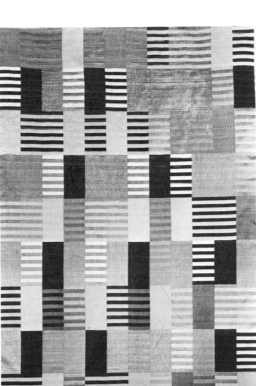
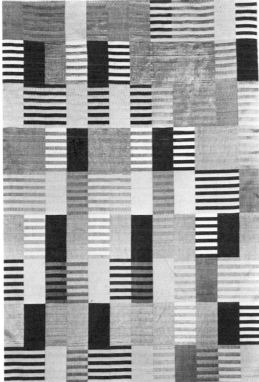

Anni Albers (1895 -). *Tapestry* (1926). Busch-Reisinger Museum, Harvard University, Purchase, German Museum Association.

89 inspiration from distorted images

Deliberate distortion* has always been present in art. Even realistic art is not true to life. In fact, the more exact everything is painted in a picture the less real it tends to become. This is because people do not see everything equally clearly: they focus their eyes on only one thing at a time.

This lesson introduces you to two of the simplest methods for creating distortions. Once you have mastered them, you can introduce distortion into your own art work to communicate ideas more intensely than would be possible otherwise.

Instructions:

1. Find a large photograph in a magazine showing a fairly simply shaped object. Mark it into equal sized squares each measuring 1". You should plan on having between 30 and 40 squares entirely filling the photograph.

2. Use a sheet of drawing paper that is larger than the photograph. Fill the paper with the same number of shapes as you drew squares on the photograph; instead of squares draw rectangles. Draw the lines, shapes, shading*, and details of what you see inside each of the squares on the photograph in the corresponding rectangles you have drawn. In this way you will both enlarge and distort the images in the photograph. The more elongated your rectangles are the more the original images will be distorted.

3. Take another large sheet of drawing paper and mark it out so that it has the same number of shapes as the original photograph. This time,

instead of drawing geometric shapes, make all the shapes irregular. Draw the lines, shapes, shading, and details seen in the squares on the corresponding irregular shapes you have just drawn. The distorted image will look very different from that of your geometric distortion. Both of these distorted images may assist you in your creative work, including the final part of this assignment.

4. Study your two distorted drawings and the original photograph. Take a clean sheet of paper and develop a finished picture based on selected parts of the photograph and the two distortions. Arrange the parts of the "realistic" and the distorted images in such a way that together they convey a fresh interpretation.

5. Submit for evaluation the photograph and the three distorted drawings.

Learning Outcomes:

1. Define distortion in reference to art work.
2. Explain how you used two different procedures to distort an image.
3. Combine two specific procedures for distorting an image to create an original work including shapes, lines, shading, and details.

Suggested Materials:

White paper; pencil and eraser; ruler

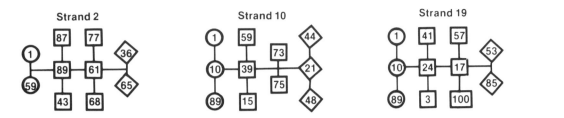

Student drawings that illustrate the techniques of distortion used in this lesson.

egyptian imagery

All cultures inherit or invent symbols*. The study of other societies often helps us enrich our personal inventories of symbols from which we draw artistic expression. In this study of ancient Egyptian art, you will learn more about a civilization that greatly influenced the art of our own culture.

In Egyptian art, people and objects are recognizable but are not shown with any attempt to achieve photographic realism. Egyptian artists followed very exact rules about ways to represent people, plants, animals, and other objects. Over many centuries a unique style* emerged that can easily be identified as Egyptian. It is not like any other artistic style.

In this lesson you are to make a careful study of an example of Egyptian art to assist you in making an art work. Artists have always learned from others when developing their own unique styles.

Egyptian (2134-1991 B.C.). *Dedu and his wife Sit-Sobk.* Limestone stela. The Metropolitan Museum of Art, Museum Excavations, 1915-16; Rogers Fund, 1916.

Instructions:

1. Study as many Egyptian paintings and bas-reliefs (very shallow carved panels) as you can find. Pottery, sculpture, and architecture can also help you; however, they are three-dimensional* and it is more difficult to visualize details from flat photographs.

2. Select one piece of ancient Egyptian art that clearly shows the characteristics of this style. Make a very careful drawing of the selected piece using line, shape, shading, and including details.

3. When the study is complete, wait for a day. Then draw the same object from memory without first looking at your study.

4. Submit for evaluation a xerox of the ancient Egyptian art work that was studied, the copy of this art work, and the drawing from memory of the art work.

Student drawing of an Egyptian vase.

Learning Outcomes:

1. List some characteristics of the style used in ancient Egyptian art.
2. Explain why artists borrow ideas from other artists whether past or present.
3. Draw an example of Egyptian art from a reproduction; draw the same example from memory.

Suggested Materials:

White paper (12" x 18"); pencil and eraser

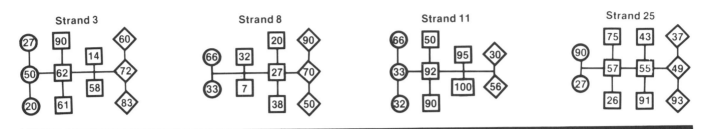

Strand 3

27 — 90 — 60
50 — 62 — 14 — 72
20 — 61 — 58 — 83

Strand 8

66 — 20 — 90
33 — 32 — 27 — 70
7 — 38 — 50

Strand 11

66 — 50 — 30
33 — 92 — 95 — 56
32 — 90 — 100

Strand 25

90 — 75 — 43 — 37
27 — 57 — 55 — 49
26 — 91 — 93

Student painting of an Egyptian mural.

189

91   logos, monograms, and trademarks

Visual symbols* surround us in just about everything we do, and they are all human inventions. Alphabetical symbols are probably the most obvious examples. But words present problems for graphic designers in that they often fill too much space or are difficult to read from a distance. As a result, designers are frequently asked to abbreviate names to initials and to put initials together in such a way that people will recognize them easily.

A design made from a person's initials is called a monogram. A company that uses its initials to identify its products will call its monogram a trademark or logo. Some groups of initials, such as UNESCO and NASA, create new words called acronyms. Many times we forget what the initials originally represented.

Here is a series of initials that we commonly see. They may help you as you work on this assignment: USA, RCA, NY, VW, NBC, GM.

Monogram designed from students' initials.

Instructions:

1. Draw the outlines of a design composed of your own initials that best suits your personality. The design is to fit comfortably on a sheet of paper measuring 12" x 18". Consider the space between the initials as well as the initials themselves. Vary the width of the shapes of the letters in your initials to add interest.

2. The design should be painted with thick creamy tempera so that the color is unchanged in appearance from one part of the design to the next. Mix enough paint for the one or more colors you decide to use. Be sure that you paint neatly up to all the lines in the monogram. Write your name and the date clearly at the bottom right of the sheet. The design should be presented as though you were a professional and were submitting it to an important client for approval.

3. Submit for evaluation a tempera painted monogram of your initials.

Learning Outcomes:

1. Define monogram, trademark or logo, and acronym.
2. Explain why your design suits your personality.
3. Design a monogram of your initials in tempera, on a 12'' x 18'' sheet of paper, that reflects your personality.

Suggested Materials:

Paper; pencil and eraser; tempera paints; brushes; mixing tray; water, paper towels

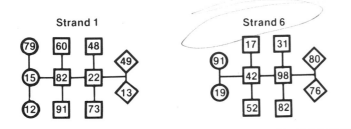

Strand 1

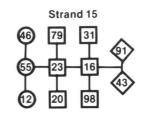

Strand 6

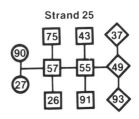

Strand 15

Strand 25

Monograms designed from students' initials.

The thousand years between the fall of Roman civilization and the European Renaissance is called the Middle Ages. The art of this period changed from century to century and from region to region, although the Roman Catholic Church enabled people to share common bonds. The Church unified Europe in ways that military leaders could not, and consequently much wealth went to support the Church. Symbols of ecclesiastical* power were evident everywhere in books, jewelry, tapestries*, paintings, mosaics*, garments, and church architecture.

Over the centuries, the wealth of the Church increased and religious art became more elaborate, providing one way to distinguish early Medieval works from more elaborate later works. Another way to distinguish Medieval art is the shape of arches used in architecture. Early work shows round or Romanesque* arches, while later work shows pointed Gothic* arches.

The task in this lesson is to learn about Medieval art by drawing examples of it.

Instructions:

1. Draw four different kinds of Medieval art from any source having good pictures. The only limitation on your choice of examples is that at least one is to show the kind of elongation of the human figure that characterizes Medieval art. Use one 9" x 12" sheet of paper for each drawing. Be sure to include all the details and shading* you can see. Clearly identify the source on each sheet.

2. Submit for evaluation all four drawings with a good photocopy of each of the original pictures used.

Carved figures from Chartres Cathedral, France.

Photo: Fred Zimmerman.

Learning Outcomes:

1. List the characteristics of Medieval art.
2. Explain the influence of the Catholic Church on art during the Middle Ages.
3. Make four drawings stressing shading and details of different kinds of Medieval art. Include one of an elongated human figure.

Suggested Materials:

White paper; pencil and eraser

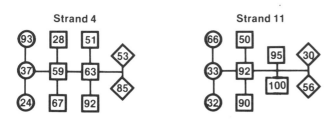

Strand 4

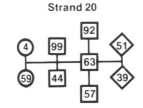

Strand 11

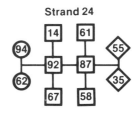

Strand 20

Strand 24

Student drawing of a medieval crucifix.

French crucifix (late 12th century). Copper and champlevé enamel. The Metropolitan Museum of Art. Gift of J. Pierpont Morgan.

93   a picture to be seen and touched

Technological advances in the textile* industry have enabled designers and manufacturers to produce a much wider variety of fabrics than ever before. Some are slick and silky-while others are coarsely woven. Textiles are works of art in their own right and yet they usually become parts of other forms of art, such as clothing, upholstery, and even constructed sculpture.

In this lesson, you are encouraged to search for examples of fabrics that have especially appealing colors and textures. You will then combine them into a collage* that invites people not only to look but also to enjoy the pleasure of touching. This experience is intended to expand your sensitivity to the range of textiles available today.

Instructions:

1. Make a collection of a wide variety of attractive and unusual fabrics from any source you can locate. Fabric shops might give you small cut-off scraps from ends of bolts of cloth. Other sources include clothing stores and furniture factories.
2. Design a collage made of a variety of contrasting fabric pieces that is to be pasted to a cardboard backing. The work is not to include recognizable objects such as plants, animals, or automobiles. The shapes are to be simplified so they can be represented by pieces of cut fabric. This will result in a non-objective* picture in which shapes and details are simplified to create new forms.

   The composition* is to focus a viewer's attention on one particular dominant* part, and yet all the parts are to be in balance.* Repeat shapes, textures, patterns, and colors to create unity*.
3. Invent a title for your collage that helps a viewer understand why you chose the fabrics that appear. Write the title on the back of the work.
4. Submit for evaluation a non-objective fabric collage.

Student textile collage.

Learning Outcomes:

1. List the different qualities of various fabrics found in your collage.
2. Explain reasons for the placement of fabric pieces in the collage with special reference to size, shape, texture, pattern, and color.
3. Create a non-objective fabric collage about a particular topic.

Suggested Materials:

Cardboard; scissors; white glue; scraps of fabric

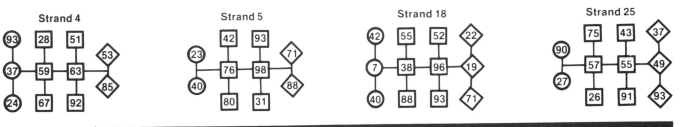

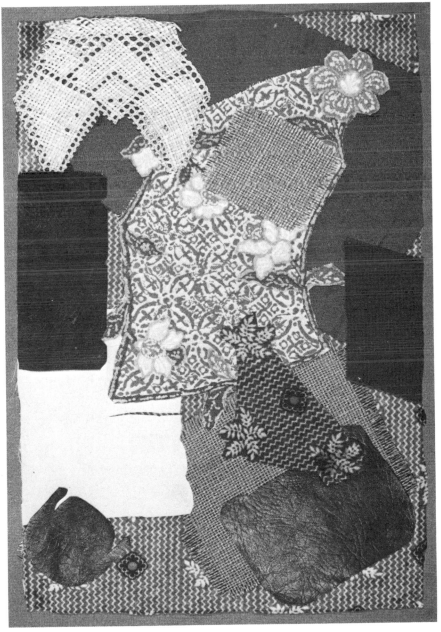

Student textile collage.

Sculpture is one kind of art that occupies real space*; it is three dimensional*. A piece of sculpture should be seen from every angle and in different lights of the day and year. It should be studied both as a whole and in detail and seen far away as well as up close. In this lesson, you are asked to go to a museum or to find sculptures in your community to study. Answering seven sets of directions about sculptures in this lesson will help you to learn to look at sculpture by focusing upon specific features.

Instructions:

1. Visit a museum that has a sculpture collection or walk through your community to find sculptures to study. Read the following and try to find sculptures that answer the directions. For each sculpture give the title, the name of the sculptor, and the date. Do not simply name sculptures, give reasons and descriptions in your answers. Keep your answers brief.

a) The technical processes sculptors use, along with their personal way of manipulating processes and materials, is called their technique. Two categories of technique are additive — that is, the sculptor adds individual pieces together to form a sculpture — and subtractive, in which the sculptor takes away material from a larger mass. Describe how the additive method is used and how the subtractive method is used in two different sculptures.

b) A sculpture is not only surrounded by space, it occupies space. Sculptures all have mass, that is they possess solidity or bulk. A sculpture need not be totally solid; it can have open and closed spaces within its mass. Describe how open and closed spaces are used in one sculpture.

c) Sculpture has a linear* direction that is defined by its axis. There is usually one dominant axis of a sculpture although several directions of movement may be present. The dominant axis may be vertical, horizontal, or diagonal. Describe the major axis in one sculpture.

d) The surfaces of a sculpture have texture that can be rough or smooth, hard or soft, deep or shallow, etc. Describe textures found in one piece of sculpture.

e) A sculpture can be one or several colors. Sometimes the sculptural material is left in its natural color and sometimes its surface is painted or treated. Describe the color in an untreated sculpture and in a treated or painted sculpture.

f) Describe a sculpture that is successful in terms of technique, space, axis, texture, and color. Describe the subject matter of this sculpture.

2. Submit for evaluation answers to six sets of directions about sculpture in a museum or in your community.

Haida Indian, Queen Charlotte Island, B.C. Canada (19th century) Coffin (front detail). Carved wood. Collection, Field Museum of Natural History, Chicago.

Benin, Nigeria (17th century). *Head of Oba.* Brass. Courtesy of the Indiana University Art Museum.

Learning Outcomes:

1. List seven classifications used to describe sculpture such as texture and color.
2. Describe sculptures in a museum or in your community by writing answers to six specific sets of directions.

Suggested Materials:

Writing paper; typing paper; paper and pen; typewriter

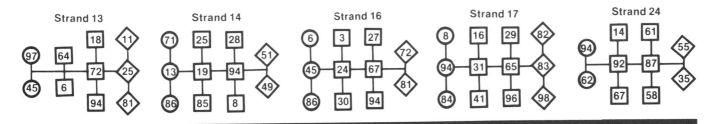

Barbara Hepworth (1903-1975). *Image.* Hopton wood stone. Barbara Hepworth Museum, St. Ives, England.

Kashmir, India (8-9th century A.D.). *Eleven-headed Avalokitesvara.* Bronze. The Cleveland Museum of Art, Purchase, Andrew R. and Martha Holden Jennings Fund.

95

describing curves

We are surrounded by objects but we are so accustomed to their presence that we are often unaware of how they look. Drawing compels us to look carefully at objects, often for the first time. The art of looking carefully helps us to understand more completely what our environment is like. Moreover, just as almost everyone can learn to read, so almost everyone can learn to draw accurately. This experience of drawing accurately, in turn, develops our visual memory.

Drawing circles and curves is often more difficult than drawing straight lines and flat surfaces. This lesson includes an introduction to drawing curves that should help you draw cylindrical objects.

Instructions:

1. A circle looks circular only when it is seen at right angles to you. At all other angles a circle appears to be flattened to make a shape called an ellipse*. The greater the angle to the viewer the flatter the circle appears.

   Before beginning this lesson draw the outline of a circular object such as a plate, a wheel, or a fry-pan from three different viewpoints. The task is to draw the different ellipses that you see as accurately as possible. While you may have some difficulty drawing evenly shaped ellipses, a greater problem lies in overcoming your knowledge that you are really looking at a circle. As a result, you will probably draw the ellipses fatter than you actually see them.

2. Next, arrange a group of five to eight food or drink cans of varied sizes, such as coke, soup, or pet food cans, into an interesting still-life*

   group. Some cans may partially overlap others, or they may be stacked on top of each other. The arrangement should also expose the ends of the cans.

3. Draw the arrangement of cans to fill a sheet of paper. Concentrate on drawing the main contours* of the cans accurately, whether fully visible or partially obscured.

4. When all the shapes have been drawn accurately, complete the still-life drawing as accurately as possible. Include all the shading you can see that shows curves and also be sure that the surface on which the cans are resting is included as well as the background that is visible.

5. Submit for evaluation the preliminary sketches of three views of a circular object and the still-life drawing of food or drink cans.

Student still-life drawing of a group of cans.

198

Learning Outcomes:

1. Define *ellipse.*
2. Explain how circles change in appearance when seen at various angles.
3. Make an accurate drawing of a still-life composed of five to eight tin cans where attention is given to the main contours and shading that describes the curvature of the cans.

95

Suggested Materials:

White paper; pencil and eraser; eight to ten cylindrical cans

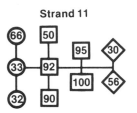

Strand 11

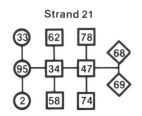

Strand 21

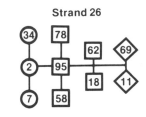

Strand 26

Student still-life drawings of groups of cans.

96

paint with matisse

Henri Matisse was one of the great artists of the first half of this century. He lived to be 85 years old and died in 1954. At the height of his career his work was characterized by simple areas of bright colors and spontaneous, brush-drawn lines, and use of bold decoration. As a student in Paris, he painted and drew realistically. By the time he was 30, however, he found that producing representational* art did not satisfy him, and he began to work with vividly colored paints making flat, pattern-like pictures similar to those created by Arab artists.

Unlike many other important artists, Matisse's painting style* never changed appreciably once he had discovered flat, patterned* painting. He continued to develop and to improve on the same ideas throughout his long life.

An artist's style can often provide clues for a person who is searching for his own individual style. In this lesson you will learn about Matisse's style by attempting to paint in that manner.

Instructions:

1. Find a book about Matisse's art in your local library and choose a colored picture of one of his paintings that appeals to you.

2. Make an accurate drawing of the picture by Matisse. Do not trace it. Now paint the picture. The colors, lines, and shapes should match the reproductions as closely as possible.

    The discipline of reproducing a picture in this way will enable you to learn much more about Matisse's art than just looking at it.

3. You are now to create an original picture and paint it. It should clearly show your interpretation of some of the main stylistic qualities found in Matisse's work.

4. Submit for evaluation your copy of a Matisse painting and a xerox of the reproduction you used, along with your own painting done in Matisse's style.

Student copy of a painting by Henri Matisse.

Learning Outcomes:

1. Explain what impressed you in Matisse's art that you felt was valuable for your own painting.
2. Paint a copy of one of Matisse's paintings as accurately as possible and paint a picture of your own in Matisse's style.

Suggested Materials:

White paper; pencil and eraser; paints; brushes; mixing tray; water, paper towels

Strand 17

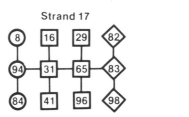

Strand 18

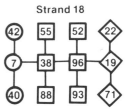

Student paintings in the style of Henri Matisse.

97

pinching a pot

The first pots were made by holding a lump of clay in one hand and pushing the thumb of the other hand deep into the clay. The clay was then squeezed between the thumb and the other fingers of that hand to make a pot-like form. This ancient technique* remains one of the foundations of pottery making today. It has been adapted to factory methods of production and it continues to be practiced by potters who specialize in hand built work.

Pinch pots tend to be quite small because they are limited in size by the hand of the potter. However, they can take on any shape the potter is able to create by squeezing the clay. Moreover, all or parts of separate pinch pots can be joined together to make larger, more sculptural objects.

This lesson instructs you on how to make a simple pinch pot. With practice your skill will develop. You will also begin to explore creative elaborations of the basic technique.

Instructions:

1. Prepare a ball of clay so that it is easy to manipulate. The clay should fit comfortably into the left hand (the right hand if you are left handed).
2. Press the thumb of the right hand (or left) deep into the clay. Squeeze the clay between the thumb and first two fingers. To begin with, squeeze with only moderate pressure.

    In order to keep water based clay in an easily workable condition, periodically wet your hands in water. The water will permeate the clay. Do not dip water based clay into water. (Oil based clay requires only the warmth from your hands to maintain its pliability.)
3. Work the fingers and thumb of your right hand around the lump of clay. At the same time, with the left hand, turn the lump to position it for squeezing. As the squeezing continues, concentrate on making the walls of the clay vessel smooth and of equal thickness. The thickness of the walls should be somewhere between ¼" and ½". Also concentrate on achieving a deep hollow form rather than a flat, open one. When you have made a satisfactory pinch pot, gently flatten the base so it will stay in one position and put it on one side to dry. Mark it with the number "1."
4. Make 5 more pinch pots that range in size from the smallest possible to the largest. Each of the five forms is to be different; each should be pleasing to you. The criterion of smooth walls of equal thickness will apply to each pot. The choice of thickness for the walls of the pinch pots will depend on the size of the piece: small pots require thinner walls than bigger ones.

    When all 6 pots have been completed, decide why they are pleasing.
5. Submit for evaluation a preliminary pinch pot and 5 others.

Paula Ahmad: Pinch pots. Courtesy of the artist.

Learning Outcomes:

1. Explain the techniques for making a pinch pot.
2. Give reasons why each of the group of five pinch pots is pleasing.
3. Make six pinch pots of various shapes and sizes.

Suggested Materials:

Water based clay (oil based clay is also satisfactory if the pots are not to be fired in a kiln); water in a bowl; paper towels; newspapers

Strand 13

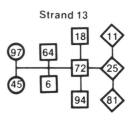

Paula Ahmad: Pinch pots. Courtesy of the artist.

Some artists and craftspersons achieve national and international recognition. Others acquire local reputations which may be just as important. During the first half of the 20th century a number of American artists became prominent because they were able to express regional feelings. Painters such as Georgia O'Keeffe, Thomas Hart Benton, Blackbear Bosin, Charles Burchfield, and Grant Wood established reputations based on paintings that showed scenes from parts of the nation where they lived.

At the same time, men and women in Kentucky, Tennessee, and New Mexico were active in crafts. Their work in woodcarving, weaving, jewelry, and ceramics became well known all across the nation.

Instructions:

1. Several examples of regional art are shown in this lesson, but you will need to search for work by artists and craftspersons from your region in your local library or museum.

2. One purpose for studying these arts and crafts is to prepare you to think about the region of the country in which you live and the unique qualities that identify it. In addition, it is hoped that you will also discover something about the artistic heritage of your area.

3. One of two tasks may be chosen to complete this lesson: either (a) make careful drawings of one art work and one piece of craft work from your region *or* (b) interview an artist or a craftsperson from your region and prepare a two to three page written statement that sums up what this person said.

4. Submit for evaluation *either* photocopies and drawings of one art and one craft object from your region *or* a report of an interview with a local craftsperson.

Thomas Hart Benton (1889-1975). *Threshing Wheat.* Sheldon Swope Art Gallery, Terre Haute, Indiana.

Learning Outcomes:

1. Explain what art qualities are found in the work of local artists or craftspersons that reflect the qualities of your part of the nation.

2. Draw an art work and a craft object by local artists or write a two to three page interview with a local artist or craftsperson.

Suggested Materials:

Drawing and/or writing materials

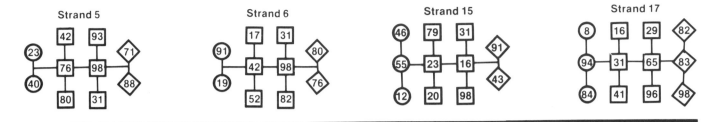

Strand 5 · Strand 6 · Strand 15 · Strand 17

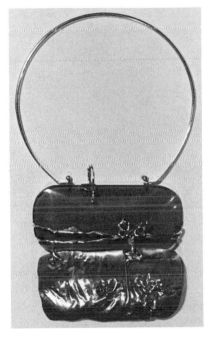

Lance Baber. Silver & acrylic necklace (1981). Courtesy of the artist.

Jenny Floch. Ceramic casserole (1981). Courtesy of the artist.

Harriet Powers. *The Creation of the Animals* (1895-98). Appliqué Quilt. Courtesy, Museum of Fine Arts, Boston. M. and M. Karolik Collection.

a ¾ view portrait

A full face view of someone shows just the symmetrical* front view. Side views and back views naturally look different. A ¾ front view is when you see someone from half way between the front and the side showing parts of both simultaneously. A good ¾ view is still balanced but it is asymmetrical and not symmetrical.

This kind of portrait work is more difficult than drawing a front or side view, but the results are much more interesting. This lesson offers you the opportunity to draw a ¾ front view portrait.

Instructions:

1. Ask a friend to pose for a portrait drawing. Position yourself so you see a ¾ front view. Sit so that your eyes are on the same level as the person posing for you. Also sit as close as possible so you can see all the important details.

2. Draw the general head shape of your friend as accurately as possible. Then mark the position of the eyes, nose, mouth, hair line, and the one ear you can see. Be sure to check and re-check these positions so you are sure they are correct. Check this planning step by looking at pictures of human skulls to see the underlying structure.

3. Add details such as eyes, nose, and mouth with *lightly* drawn lines. See page 223 for a checklist of facial proportions.

4. Shade in the portrait using several darknesses of pencil so as to achieve a full range of values. Make the whole head and all the smaller parts look as solid as possible.

5. Lastly, choose which lines should be drawn more heavily than any of the others and which parts should be shaded* more strongly. In this way you will focus the viewer's attention on the most important parts.

   Also at this time you may want to add some shading to show the color of the hair, eye brows, and eye lashes—but do not over-emphasize these parts.

6. Submit for evaluation a ¾ front view drawing of a friend.

Francoise Clouet (1510-1572). *Portrait of Claude Gouffier de Boisy.* Chalk on paper. Fogg Art Museum, Harvard University. Gift of Meta and Paul J. Sachs.

Learning Outcomes:

1. Describe the difference between ¾ front portraits and full front views.
2. Explain how the ¾ view does or does not look like your friend.
3. Draw a ¾ front portrait in proportion using a full range of dark and light values.

Suggested Materials:

White paper; 2B, 4B, 6B pencils

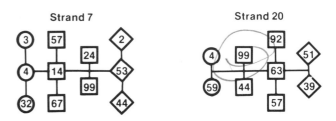

Strand 7   Strand 20

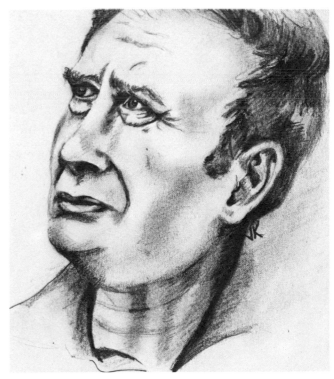

Student ¾ front view portrait drawings.

contours and drawing

A common mistake made by beginners in art is to look only at the outside edges or external contours of objects. Within most solid forms, other contours can be seen. Internal contours may, in fact, be more interesting than the outer contour or silhouette*. Sometimes it may be better for the artist to concentrate attention on the inside appearance of objects rather than on the outsides to get the best effects.

This assignment is designed to make you sensitive to the presence of internal contours.

Henri Moore. *Pink and Green Sleepers* (1941). The Tate Gallery, London.

The artist concentrated in this drawing on internal contours.

Instructions:

1. Wind thick wool or thick string around an interesting looking solid object that, if possible, is irregularly shaped. You may wrap the object in a regular or irregular manner just as long as the wool or string is touching the object at all points. Leave about ½" between the strands of wool or string so you can see the object underneath.

2. Draw the lines made by the string as it follows the surface of the object. Do this as carefully as you can. These lines reveal the internal contours of the object. You will notice that the wrapped yarn creates a rhythmic* design as it reveals the contours. Last of all, insert only the contour line that most people draw first; that is, the outline of the object.

3. Unwrap the object and make a completely new drawing of it. Use what you have learned about the contours that are present on the object, and employ shading* to show the three-dimensional* character of the object. Also add whatever details that are visible.

4. Submit for evaluation the drawing of the wrapped object and the final drawing of the unwrapped object.

Learning Outcomes:
1. Define external contour and internal contour.
2. Explain how an understanding of contours help you to make accurate drawings.
3. Draw an object and concentrate on the internal contours by following the lines created by string wrapped around it. Make a second drawing of the unwrapped object showing the internal contours by means of shading.

100

Suggested Materials:
White paper; pencil and eraser; thick wool or string; an irregularly shaped solid object

Strand 11

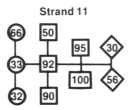

Strand 19

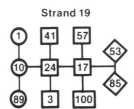

Strand 27

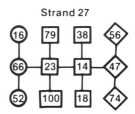

Student drawing of a horn wrapped with cord to mark the internal contours.

Student drawing of a horn showing both internal and external contours.

Guidelines for the Management of Large Group Art Instruction

This instructional manual may be used where a teacher is responsible for a few students or in conventional sized classes, although its uniqueness lies in using it when instructing large groups of students. *Artstrands* represents the culmination of over ten years of teaching, evaluation, and revision that occurred during the evolution of a general elective, studio art course designed for students of college age and older. The instructional manual for the course was revised and improved on four separate occasions prior to its use in *Artstrands*. During this period, the number of students enrolling in the course increased from 50 to over 500 per semester. Over the same period, the course has also been offered as a correspondence course with an enrollment that has grown to more than 300 students.

As a result of this course, large numbers of college students have been able to enrich their education with an art course. For lack of confidence or experience, many of these students would never have enrolled in studio art courses. Many students who have taken this course have found art interests to develop in their leisure time, and a few have discovered talents they did not realize they possessed and have gone on to more advanced art study.

Although large enrollment studio art instruction is practical, it requires special techniques of management. This section presents information to help instructors use the manual to teach art to large numbers of students.

Six topics are addressed:

1. Recruitment of students
2. Classroom space and organization
3. Instruction and evaluation
4. Student records
5. Staff selection and training
6. Professional coordination

Recruitment of Students. Many people possess a natural desire to make art; their education can be enhanced if they study art. Unfortunately, many students are unable or unwilling to take advantage of this kind of opportunity because of the constraints imposed in many education programs and the competition for grades which often interferes with broader educational goals.

The recruitment of students to this kind of art course requires that many obstacles be overcome. Anxieties about lack of ability or lack of experience must be alleviated. Students need to be advised that they can succeed in this course, but in succeeding they will be expected to make considerable effort. They need to know that consistent effort and applied skills will be measures of success in the course.

In order to recruit successfully for a course of this kind, prospective students need to be aware that this opportunity is available; this message can only be communicated through advertising. Announcements about the course can be published in student newspapers; explanatory handbills can be displayed in dormitories and distributed during registration for classes. Freshman advisors and other program advisors should receive announcements and should be asked to inform students about the course. Another effective method of publicizing the course is by means of exhibits of student art produced in the course. Exhibits, more than any other means, provide a vehicle for reaching students to reduce their anxieties about the limitations of their own abilities. However, the best method of recruitment, after the course has been offered, is word of mouth. Students who have taken the course and enjoyed a rewarding experience will pass the word on to their friends.

Typically, enrollments will gradually increase

as more and more students have successfully completed the course. The ceiling on enrollments will be governed by demand or by external factors such as funds available for staffing.

Classroom Space and Organization. When the course is taught to a conventional sized class, it is best handled in a regular studio classroom. For larger enrollments, a variety of locations may be suitable. All that is needed is a large area furnished with several tables and chairs and with additional chairs to accommodate waiting students. A dormitory lounge is an ideal location, but any large room will do as long as it has good lighting and ventilation. Perhaps the most critical decision governing the success of the course is that it be offered in a location that is well known and easy to reach.

The staff needs adequate storage space for student records, examples of student work, instructional visuals, and art supplies for use in demonstrations. Lockable cabinets are sufficient if they have deep shelving, although an adjacent storeroom is preferred.

In contrast to a course schedule, with classes held two or three times a week at specified times, the large enrollments in this course are handled most effectively when the classroom is kept open and staffed over long periods of time. Large numbers of students can then be counseled during many hours, several days every week. Individual students can visit for assistance for varying periods of time as their schedules allow. After the weekly flow of students has settled into a pattern, the number of staff members on duty can be adjusted. In the experience of the authors, for example, when a room has been open from 6pm to 9 pm, Monday through Thursday, larger numbers of students tend to come on Wednesdays and Thursdays. More instructors, therefore, should be scheduled for days that attract heavier attendance.

Many students who enroll in the course have never been taught to organize their time effectively. For their own good, they should be required to check with a staff member once a week and record their attendance. The staff can then advise students about their progress and schedule.

Because of the unusual organization of the course, attendance should be recorded and weighted as part of the grade. On the other hand, once students have completed all course requirements, they are awarded a grade and are no longer required to attend.

Although the attendance check does not require a student to bring work to be evaluated, students often bring work when they visit the room. Sometimes, the work will be in progress and students will seek advice. On other occasions, finished work will be brought in for evaluation. Students will sometimes ask for advice on such topics as what to do next or where to purchase art supplies.

Students receive individual attention each time they visit. The amount of time spent with an instructor will vary with the kind of help required and how many students are waiting to be counseled. More interested students will soon learn when they can receive more counseling.

The following rules will assist both students and instructors:

1. No more than one finished art work may be submitted on each class visit.
2. At least half the products required for each student must be submitted by the midterm of the course. As with any large enrollment course, students should be required to attend midterm and end-of-term grading sessions. We have found that alphabetic clusters (A-D; E-H; etc.) facilitate scheduling of these sessions.

Instruction and Evaluation. As explained in the introduction, students select strands of lessons and the lessons they would like to do with each strand. The work of the instructors, therefore, is generally as follows:

1. Advising students how to make strand and lesson choices.
2. Assisting with problems and proposals about choices and sources of art materials.
3. Directing students to reproductions (slides, prints, etc.) of art works that show how a completed lesson might appear. These reproductions should include examples of student work and works by famous artists.
4. Providing guidance for students who come in for consultation and help for students who bring in unfinished work.
5. Demonstrating particular skills and techniques that would help students complete or improve their work.
6. Evaluating finished student work against the criteria that appear as "Learning Outcomes" at the end of each lesson and entering a grade on the student's class record.

7. Instructing students that all art work must be unmounted when submitted. When a grade is given, the instructor will sign the back and record the date on the art work. Discovery of work previously submitted by another student should lead to severe penalty, (reduced course grade, loss of credit for that lesson, etc.).

8. Encouraging students to retain, improve, and resubmit work that has been evaluated and graded as less than A. Work that is resubmitted for a second evaluation has a good possibility of receiving a higher grade. This practice has led to evaluation consultations becoming powerful instructional tools.

9. Storing superior work to be photographed for inclusion in a slide collection of high quality student work before being returned to students. Items in this collection become an important teaching resource that should always be readily available in the classroom.

Student Records. Accurate record keeping is important in an individualized course such as this one, regardless of the size of the enrollment. For every credit hour enrolled, a student produces four art works from one strand. Therefore, for three credit hours, they are required to complete three strands consisting of 12 lessons. Instructors base their evaluation on evidence of eight hours work for each lesson completed. A reasonable amount of time is allowed for finding suitable lessons, assembling art materials, researching a topic in the library, making false starts, properly finishing works, and visiting the instructional staff for advice and evaluation. Students commonly enroll for three credit hours, although the course may be offered for one to five credit hours. Since three credit hours translates into twelve pieces of required art work, twenty students will submit 240 pieces of work that must be evaluated; 500 students leads to the submission of 6,000 pieces of work. The magnitude of this figure may seem difficult to manage, yet that is not the case. An efficient system of accurate record keeping is essential and can be achieved in the following manner:*

1. At the first class meeting, a file folder is made for each student enrolled (students can be directed to make their own folders).

*In the event that computer programs are available, records can be entered into a computer terminal and recalled on demand whenever a student comes for assistance.

2. An evaluation form (pages 214-215) with the student's name and social security number is stapled into each student's folder. The number of credit hours, based on the number of strands to be completed, is also entered.

3. Weekly attendance records are entered on the evaluation form by instructors.

4. At the first class session, all students must sign on the evaluation form that they have read the rules for the course — to be sure that they are familiar with the management of the course.

5. Grades are entered on the evaluation forms as work is evaluated. As deemed necessary, instructors' comments are also included.

6. Student folders are kept in file boxes and are never handled by students.

7. Grades for student work, completed during the first and second halves of the course, are calculated with grades assigned to weekly attendance.

8. When large numbers enroll in the course, advance notice must be given that incomplete grades are not generally possible except in extreme circumstances. This policy insures completion of the course by all students and avoids cumbersome record keeping.

Staff Selection and Training. The best staff instructors are generally undergraduate juniors or seniors who are majoring in Art Education. They are likely to be successful because they have chosen teaching as a vocation. Fine Arts majors may also make good instructors if they have knowledge and skill in art and enjoy working with people.

A typical instructor to student ratio is somewhere between 1:80 and 1:100. With a total enrollment of 500, a typical staff of between 5 to 7 is needed. Staff instructors have to be available to work the hours when the course is offered, usually two evenings a week. In the experience of the authors, the course has been most effectively offered in the evenings.

Preliminary staff training focuses on learning course rules, knowing how to prepare and maintain records, and becoming familiar with the lessons and strands in the manual. However, the heart of instructor training occurs on the job. Instructors advise students on the choice of lessons and strands, demonstrate skills, interpret lesson instructions, develop skills as evaluators, and help and encourage students to do their best possible work. All this is done as peer tutoring — a valuable experience for the instructor staff.

Evaluating art is difficult under the best of circumstances. The statements of "Learning Outcomes" provide criteria, but final judgment always rests with the instructor. Since students who enroll in this course tend to be mature, they regularly ask for justifications for their grades and will often challenge instructor decisions. Instructors, therefore, have to learn to be firm and fair. This experience often places quite severe demands on instructors. During the process, staff instructors not only assist the students enrolled in the class, they also sharpen their own evaluation skills.

Professional Coordination. Primary responsibility for the course must always lie in the hands of a qualified, professional art educator. With large enrollments, this person's task is to take responsibility for management of the course and to instruct the staff in peer tutoring and instructional counseling. The coordinator's tasks are as follows:

1. Identifying and arranging for the use of a suitably equipped room.

2. Advertising the course and establishing communications with the counselors and others who might encourage student enrollment.
3. Hiring, training, and scheduling staff instructors.
4. Ordering course manuals and preparing supplementary handouts.
5. Counseling students enrolled in the course who have special problems.
6. Supervising course record keeping.
7. Managing the course budget (staff time, course materials, and incidental expenses).
8. Assigning final grades.
9. Arranging exhibits of student art work.
10. Overseeing the preparation and availability of visual references of slides and prints.

Good Luck

Individualized instruction for large groups of students can be rewarding *and* frustrating. Successful management of large groups takes time and patience. Once organizational parts move smoothly and efficiently, the outcomes, in terms of student interest and art learning, will be most rewarding.

No. of hrs. _____

Section _____

Attendance Record and Evaluation

Student Name _____

Campus Address_____

Phone _____ Social Security No. _____ Class_____

I have read and am responsible for the content in the course syllabus.

_____
Student's Signature

Week	Date	Initials
1		
2		
3		
4		
5		
6		
7		
8		
9		
10		
11		
12		
13		
14		
15		
16		

Strand Number: _____

Date	Lesson #	Rating	Initials

Strand Number: _____

Date	Lesson #	Rating	Initials

Strand Number: _____

Date	Lesson #	Rating	Initials

Strand Number: _____

Date	Lesson #	Rating	Initials

[cont. next page]

Strand Number: _____

Date	Lesson #	Rating	Initial

Midterm Grade _____

Final Grade _____

Re-do Instructions: Initial

Lesson # _____   _____

Lesson # _____   _____

Lesson # _____   _____

Notes

Glossary

The selection of words includes those that are marked in the lessons with asterisks. In addition, other words are included that are particularly useful when using this book. The definitions have all been written for specific use with this book.

Abstract Not imitative of nature; capturing the feeling of a subject while not wholly dependent upon it.

Additive Sculpture Making sculpture by the addition of pieces where the identity of the individual pieces is often lost.

Advertising The art of printed or spoken matter that communicates a product or an idea to an audience.

Aerial (Atmospheric) Perspective The effect that colors appear to undergo with distance, where atmospheric interference affects brightness, lightness, and darkness.

Aesthetic Reflecting a sensitivity to beauty or something that is judged to be beautiful.

Appliqué The art of sewing pieces of cloth or other material to a fabric background to create a design.

Arch A curved structure made to support a wall, where an opening is needed to let people or light pass through.

Architecture The art of designing and constructing buildings; a style of construction such as "Elizabethan" architecture; the science, art, or profession of designing and constructing buildings.

Armature A skeleton-like support in sculpture made of wire, piping, metal rod, rolled paper, etc. Sculpture media such as clay, plaster, papier mâché are built around the armature.

Art Critic A person who applies rational criteria to the assessment of works of art.

Art Historian A scholar who studies the art of the past and endeavors to understand the meaning of that art.

Asymmetry A form of balance where each side of a center line has a different character (i.e., not symmetrical).

Axis A straight line around which the parts of an object or system are regularly arranged.

Background Parts of a work of art that are usually less important and more distant (see p. 223 for an illustration).

Balance Relates to the equilibrium evident in works of art.

Baroque The period in art that followed the Renaissance when artists became fascinated with the intricate, flamboyant play of light and dark forms and shapes.

Bas-relief Low relief sculpture in which figures project only slightly from the background (see relief sculpture).

Body Proportions How parts of the body are arranged in relation to each other (see p. 223 for an illustration).

Brayer A rubber roller with a handle used for applying an even coating of ink to a surface for printing.

Caricature The resemblances of personalities brought about by the exaggeration of noteworthy features such as noses, ears, and mouths.

Carve To fashion by cutting away unwanted parts.

Cast Duplication of relief or fully three-dimensional objects by means of molds.

Center of Interest The most important part of a work of art.

Classic A period at which time the greatest art of a civilization was produced; established excellence based on models originated in history at the height of a given culture, especially (in the western world) Greek and/or Roman.

Classical Style   Of or pertaining to, or in accordance with the precedents of ancient Greek and Roman art and literature (in the western world).

Clay   A plastic medium composed of a powder mixed with water or linseed oil.

Close-up View   A person or object as seen close to a viewer.

Coilpot   A clay pot constructed with a system of coils.

Collage   A work of art produced when various materials are glued to a surface.

Column   A post that supports a roof.

Complementary Colors   Colors lying directly opposite each other on the color wheel; i.e., blue and orange, red and green, etc. When mixed together they make grays or browns. When side by side they intensify each other.

Composition   The product of art where all the parts hold together to form a unified whole.

Concave   A hollow, curved form like a section of the inside of a sphere.

Contemporary   Belonging to the same period of time usually current or modern.

Content   What an art work is about, such as the subject matter.

Contour   The visible limit or edge of any shape or mass; an outline of a shape or mass.

Contrast   A pronounced difference between two things; to set in opposition in order to show a difference.

Converge   To tend or move toward one point or one another; sometimes to come together and unite in a common interest or focus.

Convex   Having a surface that curves outward like the surface of a sphere.

Cool Colors   The green and blue range of colors in the color wheel.

Craftsmanship   A concern for using tools and materials in the most skillful and appropriate way possible.

Crayon Etching   A pictorial technique where an india ink covering is scratched away with a sharp tool to reveal an underlying crayoned surface.

Create   To cause to exist, to originate, to bring about, to produce imaginatively.

Critique   A careful analysis of a work of art.

Cubism   A style of art that reduces recognizable objects to geometric forms; or often shows objects from several positions at one time; and often makes opaque forms transparent.

Decoration   The addition of surface ornamentation such as lines, colors, and shapes to enhance objects.

Depth   The condition of (a) actual distance in a work of art, or (b) the suggestion of distance (the illusion).

Design   An organized arrangement of one or more art elements such as line, texture, mass, space, value, and color.

Dimension   A measure of spatial extent in the direction of length, breadth, or depth. Two-dimensional art (drawing, painting, print making, etc.) possesses length and breadth; three-dimensional art (sculpture, architecture, jewelry, etc.) includes depth, in addition to length and breadth.

Distortion   The process of changing a shape in some way to make it more interesting and powerful by twisting it out of its proper or natural form.

Dominant   In art, the word refers to a part or parts that are of major importance.

Draw   The act of marking a surface with an instrument such as a pencil, pen, or brush that makes lines.

Drawing Paper   Paper with a surface specially adapted for drawing.

Ecclesiastical   Relating to the organization of a church.

Edition   In printmaking, the total number of prints made of a given picture or design.

Elements of art and design   The commonly recognized art elements: color, line, mass, shape, space, and texture.

Ellipse   A geometric shape which, unlike an oval with which it is often confused, possesses the same curvature at each end.

Engrave   To carve into a surface; to cut with a sharp tool into a metal plate or wooden block for printing.

Exaggerate   To enlarge something, disproportionately — to overstate.

Expressionism   Art that abandons naturalism for the greater emotional impact possible from simplified outlines and strong color.

Eye Level   An imaginary line that corresponds with the level of a person's eyes. The eye level and the horizon are the same.

Face Proportions How parts of the face are arranged in relation to each other (see p. 223 for an illustration).

Felt Pen A drawing instrument where fluid is passed through a spongy material leaving a bold line.

Final Drawing A finished drawing that is often developed from a preparatory sketch.

Fire The process of baking clay in a kiln to turn it into pottery.

Foreground The part of a work of art that appears nearest the viewer and is usually the most important part (see p. 223 for an illustration).

Foreshortening The illusionary shortening of objects to indicate depth in space. It occurs clearly when arms or tree limbs point either toward or away from the viewer.

Form The structural organization of an object mass (three-dimensional) or shape (two-dimensional) that is defined by its contour.

Free Form Non-geometric shapes usually having curved flowing contours rather than straight-sided contours.

Free Standing Sculpture Sculpture that stands without support or attachment and is designed to be looked at from any position.

Fresco The art of painting with earth colors on wet plaster; usually wall painting that has been rendered in a wet ground of fresh lime and gypsum or wet "plaster."

Full Face A full front view of a head. The entire figure may also be shown as a front view.

Functional Designed for or adapted to serve a particular useful purpose.

Geometric Figures Two-dimensional shapes and three-dimensional geometric masses such as circles, spheres, triangles, squares, cubes, and ellipsoids.

Glaze (in ceramics) A liquid suspension of finely ground materials, applied to the surface of ceramic ware; which when fired at a high temperature, melts together to form a glassy coating.

Gothic Art The arts of Western Europe between the 12th and 15th centuries.

Gradation (in color, and texture) A gradual, imperceptible change from one state to another, as in making a smooth transition from one color to another.

Greek Art The arts of Greece, such as painting, sculpture, architecture, and ceramics, usually made during the period 900 to 100 B.C.

Grid Square or rectangular divisions drawn on a sheet of paper and used as a guide for making accurate drawings.

Horizontal Relating to, and parallel with, the horizon (flat and level).

Hue The name given to blue, red, green, etc. (a less accurate but more common-place term than hue is the word color).

Image Any visual impression of a person, thing, or idea that can be drawn, painted, or sculpted.

Imaginative New images of things that have never existed or images about objects or ideas derived from combining previous experiences.

Impasto A thick or heavy application of paint.

Impressionism A 19th century French school of painting concerned with the out of doors and capturing impressions of the moment by means of painting the impact of light on surfaces.

Intensity Refers to the amount of pureness or brilliance of a hue (color).

Kiln A specialized oven designed for baking clay forms into ceramic ware.

Landscape An artistic rendering of outdoor scenes usually containing hills, trees, foliage, figures, prairie, woodland, and mountains. Specialized variations include seascapes and cityscapes.

Lettering Style The character of a given alphabet of letter forms.

Lithograph A printing process based on the principle that oil and water repel each other.

Line The mark made by a moving point that suggests a direction or an edge.

Linear Made of or using lines.

Linoleum Block In print making, linoleum provides a surface into which tools cut to reveal images that are then printed.

Logo A symbolic form, frequently composed of letter shapes, that identifies a business organization, social unit, etc.

Loom Any type of device which will permit warp threading and allow for weaving.

Lower Case The small letters of the alphabet as distinct from the upper case or capital letters.

Manuscript A hand-written document.

Mass A quantity of matter in a work of art having

definite shape and size; an object that has solidity.

Medieval Belonging to the Middle Ages usually between 500 A.D. and 1500 A.D.

Medium (plural: media or mediums) Any material used for expression or delineation in art.

Middle Ground The part of a work of art halfway between the viewer and the background (see p. 223 for an illustration).

Mixed Media A single work of art created with a mixture of art materials such as paint, collage, and prints.

Mold A hollow form which, when filled with plaster or metal, duplicates objects.

Monogram The combination of two or more letters to form a unit.

Monoprint A simple printing process that produces only one copy.

Monochromatic Color application in art using only one hue; variations are possible with the addition only of black and white to create shades and tints of the hue.

Montage A pictorial image made by cutting and gluing photographs or parts of photographs together.

Mosaic Pictures and patterns made by arranging many small, usually square, pieces side by side; when a mosaic is made of pieces of tile, glass, etc., the remaining spaces are filled with plaster-like grout.

Motif A repeated unit or figure in a design.

Mural A form of painting executed directly on walls or on surfaces, such as wood and paper, that are attached to walls.

Natural Object Present in or produced by nature; not artificial, that is, not manmade.

Negative Space Space around shapes and masses that is often explained imperfectly as background.

Non-objective A form of artistic expression that does not depict known objects.

Oil Painting A painting made with a mixture of finely ground color pigment and linseed oil, usually applied to a canvas surface.

Opaque Impenetrable by light.

Optical Illusion A deceptive appearance, an illusion due to misinterpretation of visual images.

Ornamental Something used for decoration or adornment.

Oval A round geometric shape with one end larger than the other; an egg shape.

Overlapping One shape or object covering up some part or all of another shape.

Paint A mixture of a pigment suspended in a liquid adhesive that when dry is hard and holds the pigment in place.

Paper A thin sheet of material made of cellulose pulp, derived mainly from wood and rags and used chiefly for writing, printing, drawing, wrapping, and covering walls.

Pattern Repetition of a design unit or motif.

Perspective The optical and mathematical guidelines for suggesting solid objects on a flat surface.

Pigment Finely ground powder of carefully controlled hue which when mixed with a suitable liquid adhesive (vehicle) makes paint.

Plane Any surface that is flat.

Portrait A pictorial representation of a specific person; usually a person's face.

Pose To assume or hold a particular position or posture as in sitting for a portrait.

Positive Space Shapes in a design that are usually observed before the negative space or background.

Poster An attention-attracting device designed to deliver a specific message.

Pottery Objects made from clay that are usually fired in a kiln to make them durable.

Press Type Letters, symbols, and designs that can be transferred from a prepared sheet to a surface by applying pressure.

Primary Colors Red, yellow, blue. Colors (hues) from which all other colors in the color wheel can be produced or mixed.

Print A motif or mark that typically can be repeated in identical form many times over.

Printmaking The art of impressing a surface with a motif or mark.

Profile A drawing or painting of the side view of an object; usually the outline of a human face.

Proof A term used in printing to designate a trial print.

Proportion A harmonious relation of parts or the ratios that exist between the various parts of an object.

Rasp A coarse file used for shaping wood or plaster.

Realism Faithful representation of people and things that seeks to capture the spirit of real things as well as the appearance of reality.

Relief Sculpture Work that projects from a surface and ranges from being almost flat (bas relief) to projecting to the point that it stands almost wholly free.

Renaissance The period that began in Italy and took place from the 14th to the 17th centuries.

Rendering A synonym for painting or drawing usually associated with architectural, advertising, and industrial design work.

Repetition An act of repeating, saying, or doing something over and over again.

Representation To depict a likeness or image of something realistically.

Rhythm Lines and shapes that are made to happen repeatedly in the same or a similar way and suggest flowing movement.

Roman Art The art of antiquity from 300 B.C. to 400 A.D. in those regions dominated by Rome; very strongly influenced by Greek art.

Romanesque The period between 800 A.D. to 1200 A.D.; art and architecture characterized by round arches, thick vaulting, massive walls, interior bays, paintings of religious items, mosaics, and story telling.

Romantic Refers to art that is exotic and reflects the unbridled expression of passions.

Rubber Cement A rapidly drying elastic substance used for joining paper and other materials. It does not penetrate, wrinkle, or stain paper, and the paper can easily be separated without tearing.

Scene The setting or locale in which any event, real or imagined, occurs.

School In art, the word school refers to a group of artists who work in very much the same way at the same period of time.

Screenprint A stencil process where the design is adhered to a stretched screen of silk-like fabric.

Sculpt The act of modeling, carving, or constructing sculpture.

Secondary Colors Orange, violet, and green colors made by mixing two primary colors (hues) together.

Self-portrait A sculpture, painting, drawing, or photograph of oneself.

Serigraph Another term for a screenprinting; often used for pictorial images.

Shade A hue with the addition of black (also called tone).

Shading To express light and dark in a drawing by darkening some parts and leaving others light.

Shape Anything flat that is cut or drawn on a piece of paper; that which is enclosed by line or an area of color.

Sign A visible mark that has an accepted meaning.

Silhouette A profile or outline of a person or object.

Sketch A simple rough drawing or design that is done rapidly and without much detail, usually made in preparation for a larger finished product.

Slip A creamy mixture of clay and water used for joining pieces of clay together and also as surface decoration.

Solid Offering resistance to pressure; filled with matter; thick, dense; having three dimensions.

Space The distance, interval, or area between or within solid or tangible forms.

Stencil A sheet of material in which a design has been cut, and through which ink or paint is squeezed or brushed to transfer an image.

Still Life Arrangement of inanimate objects that becomes the subject matter for artistic expression.

Stitchery The art of creating images by means of such materials as wool, thread, and string stitched to a textile backing.

Style The manner or mode of expression, execution, construction, or design in art that may be personal or reflect a particular set of standards.

Subject Something dealt with in a specific way in writing, music, and painting; the main theme or leading figure.

Subordinate In art, the word refers to a part or parts that are of lesser importance than other parts.

Subtractive Sculpture Making sculpture by removing material from an original mass (carving).

Surface The outer part of anything having length and breadth.

Surreal Depicting images of the kind associated with dreams and hallucinations.

Symbol In art, a graphic letter, figure, or sign that represents or suggests an object or idea.

Symmetry A form of balance where both sides of a center line reveal the same character (i.e., not asymmetrical).

Tapestry   A fabric with designs woven into the material.

Technique   A particular way of performing a task.

Tempera Paint   An opaque painting medium in which coarsely ground pigments are mixed with an adhesive (vehicle) of water and gum.

Tesserae   Small, approximately square, pieces of material, such as marble, glass, and tile used for making mosaics.

Textile Art   The application of designs on or in a fabric to create a work of art.

Texture   The actual or visual quality of a surface that may be rough, smooth, silky, etc.

Three Dimensional   Exhibiting the three dimensions of length, breadth, and depth.

Tint   The addition of white to a hue.

Trademark   Registered name, symbol, or sign usually used to distinguish one manufacturer's goods and services from others.

Transparent   Permits rays of light to pass through to allow images behind or beneath to be seen clearly.

Translucent   Permits the passage of light, but with little or no clear imagery to be seen behind or beneath.

Two Dimensional   Exhibiting the two dimensions of length and breadth.

Unity   The degree to which all the parts of a work of art hold together in a state of oneness; when something looks as though all the parts belong together.

Upper Case   The capital letters of the alphabet.

Value   In art, value refers to the lightness or darkness of different hues and degrees of lightness and darkness in a hue.

Vanishing Point   A point used as a guide on an imaginary horizon where receding parallel lines seem to come together or converge.

Vertical   Relating to, and perpendicular with the horizon (straight up and down).

Warm Colors   The red and yellow range of colors on the color wheel.

Warp   Vertical threading of a loom, resulting in threads through which the weft is woven.

Wash   A watery paint mixture applied to paper to fill a space, usually a background.

Water Color   A transparent painting medium in which finely ground pigments are mixed with an adhesive (vehicle) of water and gum.

Weave   The interlacing of thread or yarn to make fabric.

Weft   The thread, yarn, etc., that is woven back and forth across the warp threads to make the visible designs of a textile.

Wet Brush   A technqiue in painting which requires that the work be done with a brush heavily loaded with thin watery paint.

Woodcut   A print made from a block of wood into which a picture or design has been cut.

X-acto Knife   A small, versatile cutting tool with replaceable razor-like blades.

Yarn   Strand-like fiber composed of cotton, wool, or synthetic material that is used in a variety of art forms such as stitchery, weaving, appliqué, collage, and sculpture.

Approximate Proportions of Heads and Bodies

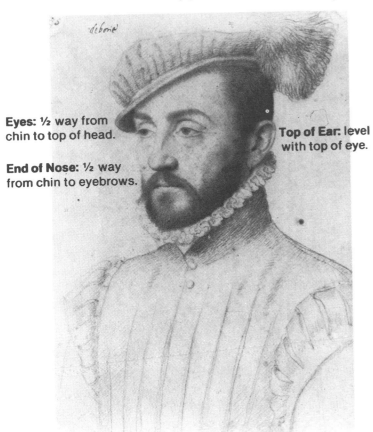

Eyes: ½ way from chin to top of head.

End of Nose: ½ way from chin to eyebrows.

Top of Ear: level with top of eye.

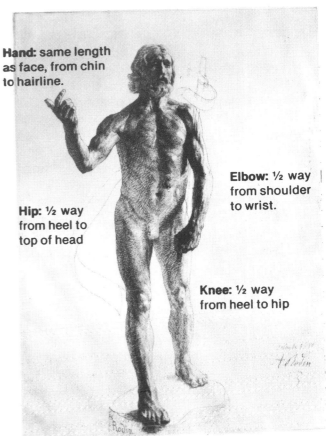

Hand: same length as face, from chin to hairline.

Elbow: ½ way from shoulder to wrist.

Hip: ½ way from heel to top of head

Knee: ½ way from heel to hip

Parts of Pictures

Mountains in background.

Houses and fields in middleground.

Large trees in foreground.